PEEPOLYKUS WITH LIVERPOOL EVERYMAN & PLAYHOUSE, NUFFIELD, BRISTOL OLD VIC

- T

MAS...E

TRAGEDY OF

MADAME BOVARY!

GUSTAVE FLAUBERT'S COMPLEX NOVEL
LOVINGLY DERAILED BY PEEPOLYKUS
ADAPTED BY JOHN NICHOLSON & JAVIER MARZAN

First performed at the Everyman, Liverpool, on 6 Feb 2016

LIVERPOOL

Nuffield

Bristol Old Vic

ROYAL
DERNGATE &
NORTHAMPTON

The Massive Tragedy of Madame Bovary

A new adaptation by **John Nicholson** & **Javier Marzan**
Based on the novel by **Gustave Flaubert**

Cast

Emma Bovary, 'Emma Fielding' and as cast	**Emma Fielding**
Charles Bovary, 'John Nicholson' and as cast	**John Nicholson**
'Javier Marzan' and as cast	**Javier Marzan**
'Jonathan Holmes' and everything else	**Jonathan Holmes**

Company

Director	**Gemma Bodinetz**
Set Designer	**Conor Murphy**
Costume & Associate Designer	**Amanda Stoodley**
Lighting Designer	**Jack Knowles**
Sound Designer	**Fergus O'Hare**
Composer	**Peter Coyte**
Assistant Director	**Anthony Almeida**
Production Managers	**Sean Pritchard** & **Jeff Salmon**
Costume Supervisor	**Jacquie Davies**
Company Manager	**Sarah Lewis**
Stage Manager at Everyman	**Kate Foster**
Company Stage Manager at Nuffield, Bristol Old Vic and Royal & Derngate	**Gemma Dunne**
Deputy Stage Manager at Everyman	**Roxanne Vella**
Deputy Stage Manager at Nuffield, Bristol Old Vic and Royal & Derngate	**Steph Carter**
Assistant Stage Manager	**Stacy Armstrong**
Technical ASM	**Antony Claas**
Wardrobe Manager	**Laura Hollowell**

Cast

EMMA FIELDING | EMMA BOVARY, 'EMMA FIELDING' AND AS CAST

Emma is Associate Artist at the Royal Shakespeare Company. **Theatre credits include:** *Rapture Blister Burn* (Hampstead); *In the Republic of Happiness* and *Spinning into Butter* (Royal Court); *Decade* (Headlong); *The King's Speech* (Wyndham's Theatre); *Heartbreak House* (Chichester); *Playing With Fire, Look Back in Anger* and *Arcadia* (National Theatre); *Rock 'n' Roll* (Duke of York's); *Macbeth, Heartbreak House, 1953* and *School for Wives* (Almeida); *Cymbeline, Measure For Measure, The School for Scandal* [Olivier Award nomination], *Twelfth Night, A Midsummer Night's Dream* and *The Broken Heart* (Royal Shakespeare Company); *Private Lives* [Oliver Award nomination & New York Theatre World Award] (Albery Theatre & Broadway) and *Jane Eyre* (Sheffield Crucible). **Film credits include:** *Fast Girls, Twenty8k, The Other Man, Discovery of Heaven, Pandaemonium, The Scarlet Tunic* and *The Great Ghost Rescue*. **Television credits include:** *Dark Angel, Close to the Enemy, Capital, Arthur & George, This Is England '90, New Tricks, Foyle's War, DCI Banks, Silk, The Game, George Gently, Father Brown, Death In Paradise, The Suspicions of Mr Whicher, Kidnap and Ransom, Midsomer Murders, The Cranford Chronicles, Fallen Angel, Ghost Squad, Beneath the Skin, The Government Inspector, Waking the Dead, My Uncle Silas, Birthday Girl, Big Bad World, The Inspector Lynley Mysteries, Other People's Children, A Respectable Trade, The Mrs Bradley Mysteries, A Dance to the Music of Time, Drover's Gold, Poirot, The Maitlands, Dread Poet's Society, Tell Tale Hearts* and *The Gist*. Emma also has numerous radio broadcast credits.

JOHN NICHOLSON | CHARLES BOVARY, 'JOHN NICHOLSON' AND AS CAST / CO-ADAPTER / CO-ARTISTIC DIRECTOR OF PEEPOLYKUS

Theatre credits as a performer include ten touring shows for Peepolykus: *No Wise Men* (Liverpool Playhouse); *The Arthur Conan Doyle Appreciation Society* (Traverse); *The 13 Midnight Challenges of Angelus Diablo* (Royal Shakespeare Company); *Spyski, Jekyll and Hydish* (Lyric Hammersmith) and *The Hound of the Baskervilles* (West Yorkshire Playhouse/West End). **Television credits as a performer include:** *Under Surveillance, The Wrong Door, The Bearded Ladies, A Salted Nut, Brian Gulliver's Travels, Marley was Dead, Baskervilles, A Trespasser's Guide to the Classics (series 1 and 2)* and *Benidorm*. **Theatre credits as a writer include:** *The Hound of the Baskervilles* (West Yorkshire Playhouse/West End); *The First Thing That Ever Happened* (Lyric Hammersmith); *Nina Conti in Dolly Mixtures* and *Richard III's Rampage* (Kevin Spacey Foundation); *The Arthur Conan Doyle Appreciation Society* (Traverse, Edinburgh); *Origins* (Pentabus); *The Light Princess* (Tobacco Factory Bristol); *Dick Tracy* (Le Navet Bete) and *Shaun the Sheep stage show* (Aardman). **Television credits as a writer include:** *Off Their Rockers*. **Radio credits as a writer include:** *Marley was Dead, Baskervilles, Rik Mayall's Bedside Tales* and *A Trespasser's Guide to the Classics*.

JAVIER MARZAN | 'JAVIER MARZAN' AND AS CAST / CO-ADAPTER / CO-ARTISTIC DIRECTOR OF PEEPOLYKUS

Trained: L'École Phillipe Gaulier. **Other theatre credits include:** *No Wise Men* (Peepolykus/ Liverpool Playhouse); *Sex and the Three Day Week* (Liverpool Playhouse); *The Ghost Train* (Royal Exchange, Manchester); *Romeo and Juliet* (The Rose); *The Arthur Conan Doyle Appreciation* (Traverse, Edinburgh); *And the Horse You Rode In On* (Barbican); *Royal Jelly* (David Pugh Productions); *The Critic* (Minerva Chichester); *Spyski* (Lyric Hammersmith/West Yorkshire Playhouse); *A Streetcar Named Desire* (Nuffield); *Beauty and the Beast* (Told By an Idiot/Lyric Hammersmith/Warwick Arts Centre); *The Hound of the Baskervilles* (Duchess); *All in the Timing* (international tour); *Mindbender* (national tour); *Aladdin* (Told By an Idiot/Lyric Hammersmith); *Jack and the*

Beanstalk, A Christmas Carol and *Cinderella* (Lyric Hammersmith); *Rhinocerous* (national tour); and *Goose Nights* (international tour). **Television credits include:** *Benidorm, Watson and Oliver* (series two), *Mongrels, Royal Jelly, Clone, Comedy Connections* and *Extra*. **Film credits include:** *Paddington Bear, Acts of Godfrey* and *Not Waving But Drowning*. **Radio credits include:** *The History Play: Maggie Heart Galtieri, The Hound of the Baskervilles, Beautiful Dreamers, Cabin Pressure* and *Marley Was Dead*.

JONATHAN HOLMES | 'JONATHAN HOLMES' AND EVERYTHING ELSE

Theatre credits include: *Bah Humbug!* (SFU Woodwards, Vancouver); *The King and I* and *Crazy for You* (Gateway, Vancouver); *Brief Encounter* (Kneehigh/Vancouver Playhouse); *Red Light Winter* (Havana, Vancouver); *The Thing About Men* (Vancouver Arts Club); *Jubilee, One Touch of Venus, DuBarry Was a Lady* and *By Jupiter* (Discover the Lost Musicals/Barbican) and *L'Amfiparnaso* (Trestle). **Film credits include:** *The BFG, Rembrabdt's J'Accuse, Nightwatching, Partition, Martian Child, Helen*. **Television credits include:** *The Descendants, Almost Human, Rogue, Cult, Once Upon a Time, Fringe, Snow 2, Psych, Terminal City, Reunion, Young Blades, The 4400, Saved, Stargate Atlantis, Stargate SG1* and *Cold Squad*.

Company

GEMMA BODINETZ | DIRECTOR

Gemma Bodinetz has been the Artistic Director for the Liverpool Everyman & Playhouse theatres since 2003. Since then, she has directed *Twelfth Night, Macbeth, The Kindness of Strangers, The Mayor of Zalamea* and *Intemperance* at the Everyman and *Educating Rita, Juno and the Paycock, The Misanthrope, A Streetcar Named Desire, Tartuffe, The Hypochondriac, No Wise Men, Ma Rainey's Black Bottom, Who's Afraid of Virginia Woolf?, The Lady of Leisure* and *All My Sons* at the Playhouse and *Yellowman* on tour. Gemma previously worked at the Royal Court Theatre, London, leaving briefly to assist Harold Pinter on *The Caretaker* before returning to co-direct *Hush* with Max Stafford-Clark. She then moved on to become a freelance director and Associate Director at Hampstead Theatre. **Other directing credits include:** *Caravan* and *A Buyer's Market* (Bush); *Yard Gal* (Royal Court, London/MCC New York); *Breath, Boom* (Royal Court); *Hamlet* (Bristol Old Vic); *Luminosity* (Royal Shakespeare Company); *Rosencrantz and Guildenstern are Dead* and *Four Nights in Knaresborough* (West Yorkshire Playhouse); *Paper Husband, Chimps, English Journeys, Snake* and *After the Gods* (Hampstead); *Shopping and Fucking* (New York Theatre Workshop); *Closer to Heaven* (West End) and *Guiding Star* (Everyman, Liverpool/National Theatre).

CONOR MURPHY | SET DESIGNER

Winner of the World Stage Design bronze medal for exceptional achievement in 2013. **Theatre and dance credits include**: *Educating Rita* and *Juno and the Paycock* (Liverpool Playhouse); *The Stick House* (Raucous); *Richard III* (West Yorkshire Playhouse), *The Government Inspector, The Resistible Rise of Arturo Ui, The Crucible, Woman and Scarecrow* and *The Rivals* (Abbey, Dublin); *The Playboy of the Western World* and *Major Barbara* (Royal Exchange, Manchester); *The Birthday Party* (Bristol Old Vic); *Summer Begins* (Donmar Warehouse); *Hoors* (Traverse); *The Real Thing* (Gate, Dublin); *Attempts on her Life, Dream of Autumn* and *Life is a Dream* (Rough Magic, Dublin); *Labyrinth of Love* (Rambert); *The Four Seasons* (Birmingham Royal Ballet); *A Midsummer Night's Dream, Giselle Re-Loaded* and *Carmen* (Donlon Dance Company). **Opera credits include:** *Orphée et Eurydice* (Royal Opera House, Covent Garden); *Lohengrin* (Royal Swedish Opera); *Powder Her Face* (Royal Opera House, De Vlaamse Opera); *Salome*

(Montpellier and Korean National Opera); *The Magic Flute* (Korean National Opera); *La bohème, Wake* and *Turn of the Screw* (National Reisopera, Holland); *I Puritani* and *The Marriage of Figaro* (Grange Park Opera); *La Clemenza di Tito* (Opera North and Nancy); *L'Heure espagnole* and *Gianni Schicchi* (Wiesbaden); *The Rape of Lucretia* and *The Rake's Progress* (Angers Nantes Opera, Saint-Étienne, De Vlaamse Opera); *Un ballo in maschera* and *Der fliegende Holländer* (Opera Zuid); *Greek* (Queen Elizabeth Hall); *The Country of the Blind* (Aldeburgh Festival) and the world premieres of *Facing Goya* (Santiago de Compostela) and *Die Versicherung* (Darmstadt). **Current projects include:** *West Side Story* (Johannesburg); *Salome* (Cape Town Opera); *Tomorrow* (Rambert) and *Elektra* (Gothenburg Opera).

AMANDA STOODLEY | COSTUME & ASSOCIATE DESIGNER

Amanda trained at Liverpool Institute for Performing Arts and graduated with a first class honours degree in theatre and performance design, having previously studied and worked in illustration, graphic and interior design. **Credits for theatre, opera and exhibition include:** *Wish You Were Here* (Everyman, Liverpool) and *Canary* [assistant designer] (Liverpool Playhouse); *A Raisin in the Sun* (Eclipse/Sheffield Theatres); *The Effect* (Sheffield Crucible); *Untold Stories* (West Yorkshire Playhouse); *Anon* (Welsh National Opera); *The Masque of Anarchy* (Manchester International Festival); *Manchester Sound: The Massacre* and *Manchester Lines* – winner of Best Design, Theatre Award UK 2012 (Manchester Library Theatre); *Fireface* (JMK Award, Young Vic Theatre); *Hamlet, Black Roses* – winner of Best Studio Production, Manchester Theatre Awards 2013, *Two, Winterlong* (also Soho), *Making An Exhibition Of Ourselves* (At Home) and *Truth About Youth Festival* (Royal Exchange, Manchester); *The Family Way, Private Lives, Duet for One, Separation, Can't Pay? Won't Pay!* and *Robin Hood* (Octagon, Bolton); *The Maw Broon Monologues* (Tron, Glasgow); *Epstein* (Epstein, Liverpool/Leicester Square); *I Know Where the Dead Are Buried* (24:7 Theatre Festival, Manchester); *Dark Side of the Building* (Unity, Liverpool); *Innovasion – Liverpool Biennial* (Hope Street Ltd.) and *Four Corners* (Bluecoat Arts Centre, Liverpool). **Co-design and assistant design credits include:** *Beautiful Thing, Doctor Faustus, 1984, Blithe Spirit, Pub* and *Three Sisters* (Royal Exchange, Manchester); *Basket Case* (Royal & Derngate); *Lucia Di Lammermoor* (Grand Opera Houston); *Faith Healer* (The Sydney Festival); *Top of the World* (Spike Theatre – on tour); *Cat on a Hot Tin Roof* (Novello) and *Momo* (Stadttheater Bern).

JACK KNOWLES | LIGHTING DESIGNER

Jack trained at the Central School of Speech and Drama. **Theatre credits include:** *The Haunting of Hill House* (Liverpool Playhouse); *Wit* (Royal Exchange, Manchester); *Dan and Phil: The Amazing Tour is Not on Fire* (national tour/London Palladium); *Travelling on One Leg* and *Happy Days* (Deutsches Schauspielhaus Hamburg); *Phaedra* (Enniskillen International Beckett Festival); *The Skriker* (Manchester Internation Festival/Royal Exchange, Manchester); *Carmen Disruption* and *Game* (Almeida); *2071* (Royal Court); *The Forbidden Zone* (Salzburg Festival/Schaubühne, Berlin); *Hopelessly Devoted* (Paines Plough); *The Kilburn Passion* and *The Riots* (Tricycle); *Sorrow Beyond Dreams* (Burgtheater, Vienna); *Blink* (Traverse/Soho/international tour); *Lungs* and *Yellow Wallpaper* (Schaubühne, Berlin); *There Has Possibly Been An Incident* (Royal Exchange, Manchester/UK tour); *Moth* (HighTide/Bush); *The Changeling* (Young Vic, with James Farncombe); *Grounded* (Deafinitely Theatre); *Tommy* (Prince Edward); *Night Train* (Halle Kalk, Schauspiel Köln); *If That's All There Is* (international tour); *Red Sea Fish* (59E59 New York); *In a Pickle* (RSC/Oily Cart); *Ring-A-Ding-Ding* (Unicorn/New Victory, New York/Oily Cart); *Land of Lights, Light Show, There Was an Old Woman, The Bounce* and *Mr & Mrs Moon* (Oily Cart).

FERGUS O'HARE | SOUND DESIGNER

Theatre credits include: *No Wise Men* (Peepolykus/Liverpool Playhouse); *Educating Rita, The Misanthrope, A Streetcar Named Desire, Tartuffe* and *Our Country's Good* (Liverpool Playhouse); *Hope Place, Twelfth Night, Macbeth, The Electric Hills, Intemperance* and *Guiding Star* (Everyman, Liverpool); *The Rehearsal, Way Upstream, Someone Who'll Watch Over Me, An Ideal Husband, Uncle Vanya* and *King Lear* (Chichester Festival Theatre); *The Wars of the Roses* (Rose Theatre); *Volpone* (Royal Shakespeare Company); *Closer* (Donmar Warehouse); *The Wasp, Tiger Country* (Hampstead); *Dancing at Lughnasa, Punk Rock* and *Pentecost* (Lyric Belfast); *The Things We Do For Love* (Theatre Royal Bath); *Relative Values* (Pinter); *Daytona* (Haymarket); *Another Country* (Trafalgar Studios); *In the Next Room or The Vibrator Play* (St. James); *Passion Play* (Duke of York's); *The Winslow Boy* (Old Vic/Roundabout); *Street Scene* (Théâtre du Châtelet, Paris/ Gran Teatro del Liceu, Barcelona); *Macbeth* (NTS/Barrymore. Drama Desk nominee. Broadway World Award); *No Quarter* (Royal Court); *The Arthur Conan Doyle Appreciation Society* (Traverse); *Glasgow Girls* (National Theatre of Scotland/Citz/Theatre Royal Stratford East);

Romeo and Juliet (Corcadorca at Cork Opera House); *A Chorus of Disapproval* (Pinter); Opening Ceremony of the 2012 London Paralympic Games (Olympic Park, Stratford).

PETER COYTE | COMPOSER

Theatre credits include: *No Wise Men* (Peepolykus/Liverpool Playhouse); *Educating Rita, Juno and the Paycock, The Misanthrope* and *A Streetcar Named Desire* (Liverpool Playhouse); *Twelfth Night* and *Macbeth* (Everyman, Liverpool); *The Swallowing Dark* (Liverpool Playhouse Studio); *Spyski!* and *All in the Timing* (Peepolykus); *Shaun The Sheep stage show, Mon Droit* (Mike McShane/John Nicholson); *Voyager* (Natural Theatre Company); *Throat, Philomena's Feast, Night and Day/Spike Islands, Rope, Loser* and *Drowning Not Waving* (Company FZ/John-Paul Zaccarini). **Film soundtracks include:** *The Dream of Shahrazad* (dir. Francois Verster); *Nina Conti – Dollymixtures, DVD, Love in the Post* (dir. Joanna Callaghan); *Widowman* (dir. David Sant); *Do Not Read This, Sea Point Days, The Mothers' House* and *When the War is Over* (dir. François Verster); *Fun* (dir. Rafal Zielinski) and *John Aldus – the Spirit of the Place* (dir. Nadia Haggar). **Dance credits include work with:** Fertile Ground, Dora Frankel Dance Company, Carolyn Dorfman Dance Company, Gravity & Levity, Susan Lewis, Kirsty Little and The Wrong Size. He is also a member of the experimental improvising ensemble Automatic Writing Circle.

ANTHONY ALMEIDA | ASSISTANT DIRECTOR

As Director, theatre credits include: *privileges* (5 Plays, Young Vic); *Fox* (Southwark Playhouse); *Thousand Words* (Park); *Centre Spread* (Wardrobe); *London 2012: Glasgow* (Theatre Uncut, Trinity Centre); *Yesterday* (Theatre Uncut, Bristol Old Vic); *The Changeling* (Young People's Project, Young Vic) and *A Vampire Story* (Outreach, Bristol Old Vic). **As Associate Director, theatre includes:** *Oresteia* (Almeida/Trafalgar) and *The Odyssey* and *The Iliad* (Almeida). **As Assistant Director, theatre includes:** *Game* (Almeida); *To Kill a Mockingbird* (Regent's Park Open Air/UK tour) and *Cinderella: A Fairytale* (Tobacco Factory).

Peepolykus

Peepolykus have been creating comic theatre with proven national and international appeal for twenty years. The style of work crosses age, language and cultural boundaries. Since 1996 the artistic directors have been John Nicholson, Javier Marzan and David Sant. Peepolykus has exported its particular brand of humour to over a hundred towns and cities across four continents including Australia, The Philippines, Brunei, Columbia, Hong Kong, Singapore, India, Bangladesh, Turkey, Cyprus, Spain, Germany, Switzerland, Belgium, Barbados, Ireland, Iran, Greece, South Korea, Finland, Hungary and Holland. During this period the company has received three theatre awards, been regularly selected for the British Council's showcase at the Edinburgh Festival, transferred *The Hound of the Baskervilles* to the West End, and collaborated on numerous theatre projects and co-productions with other companies and organisations including: Neal Street Productions, Lyric Hammersmith, West Yorkshire Playhouse, Liverpool Everyman & Playhouse, Traverse Theatre, Pentabus, Bath Festival, Tobacco Factory Theatres, National Youth Theatre, National Youth Music Theatre: UK, The World Famous, The National Theatre, The Kevin Spacey Foundation, Situations, BBC and the RSC.

Peepolykus shows include: *Let the Donkey Go* (1996/97); *I am a Coffee* (1997/98); *Horses for Courses* (1998/99); *Goose Nights* (2000); *Midsummer Rude Mechanicals* for the RNT (2001); *Rhinoceros* (2002); *Mindbender* (2003); *All in the Timing* (2004/5); *The Hound of the Baskervilles* (2006-7); *Spyski* (2008-9); *No Wise Men* (2010-11); *The Arthur Conan Doyle Appreciation Society* (2012-13); *Jekyll and Hyde* (2013); Associates on *The Light Princess* (2015-16) plus *The Hound of the Baskervilles* and an adaptation of *A Christmas Carol* for BBC Radio4 (2010).

Their radio series *A Trespasser's Guide to the Classics* has just been recommissioned by the BBC. The company are also in the second phase of 'STUCK', a large-scale project researching the impact of improvisation in schools.

Peepolykus's producer is Eleanor Lloyd, to contact them regarding collaborations/licensing on other titles, please visit peepolykus.com or email eleanor@elproductions.co.uk Follow them on twitter @Peepolykus and search for Peepolykus on YouTube to watch excerpts of the company's productions.

Liverpool Everyman & Playhouse

Two Great Theatres. One Creative Heart.

We are two distinct theatres, almost a mile apart, which together make up a single artistic force.

For over ten years we have been driven by our passion for our art form, our love of our city and our unswerving belief that theatre at its best transforms lives. While our two performance bases could hardly be more different, they are united by our commitment to brilliant, humane, forward-thinking theatre that responds to its time and place.

Our mission is to reflect the aspirations and concerns of our audiences, to dazzle and inspire them, welcome and connect with them, nurture the artists within them and fuel their civic pride. Wherever these connections happen – whether in our theatres, in the community, in schools, or outside Liverpool – we hope to ignite the imagination, explore what it is to be human and always to exceed expectation.

We are two buildings with many audiences and communities, brought together by a sincere belief that theatre at its best transforms lives. This ethos was praised by the judges when the Everyman was awarded the 2014 RIBA Stirling Prize for architecture.

everymanplayhouse.com | 0151 709 4776

Nuffield

Nuffield

Nuffield is a multi-award-winning professional producing theatre company based in Southampton. It has a reputation for innovation and quality, creating bold and distinctive theatre that attracts the highest calibre of artist. Last year Nuffield won 'Regional Theatre of the Year' at The Stage Awards 2015 and the Best Design UK Theatre 2015 for *The Hudsucker Proxy*.

Led by Samuel Hodges and supported by a team of associates – directors Blanche McIntyre, Natalie Abrahami and Michael Longhurst, designer Tom Scutt and playwright Adam Brace – Nuffield's mission is to create fresh, vital experiences through theatre which invigorate and inspire.

Nuffield is also developing. It is the operating company of the North Building in Southampton's new city-centre arts complex which is due to open next year and will include a flexible 447-seat main-house theatre, a 135-seat studio, screening facilities, rehearsal and workshop spaces. This new venue will transform Nuffield's ability to show new and exciting high-quality professional work from local, national and international artists. It will also allow the programme to include dance, film and music. Nuffield will run the new city-centre venue and its existing theatre on the University of Southampton's Highfield Campus.

nuffieldtheatre.co.uk | 023 8067 1771

Bristol Old Vic

Bristol Old Vic is the oldest continuously-working theatre in the UK.

Its mission is to create pioneering twenty-first century theatre in partnership with the people of Bristol; inspired by the history and magical design of the most beautiful playhouse in the country.

Bristol Old Vic is led by artists who see the world with distinctive clarity and whose ability to articulate what they see allows us to understand and engage with our world afresh. The company's programme includes original production, artist development and outreach; its work connecting on a local, national and international level.

In 2016, Bristol Old Vic will reach its 250th birthday, celebrating with a season of work that both draws from the theatre's history and looks towards its future.

Added to which, work will shortly begin on the final phase of the building's capital development, delivering a new foyer and studio theatre designed by Stirling Prize-winning architects Haworth Tompkins.

bristololdvic.org.uk | 0117 949 3993

Royal & Derngate, Northampton

Royal & Derngate, Northampton, is the main venue for arts and entertainment in Northamptonshire. Last year more than 300,000 people saw shows and films at Royal & Derngate and another 71,000 saw co-produced work across the country, with the theatre winning the award for Best Presentation of Touring Theatre in the UK Theatre Awards 2015 for its *Made in Northampton* work. Recent years have seen the increased profile of Royal & Derngate as one of the major producing venues in the country, including being named Regional Theatre of the Year by the inaugural Stage 100 Awards in 2011, an accolade for which it has been nominated again this year.

Highlights of its *Made in Northampton* 2016 season include the first major revival of Peter Whelan's *The Herbal Bed*, a major tour of *King Lear*, starring Michael Pennington, and the world premiere of *Soul*, a new play about Marvin Gaye, by Roy Williams.

Royal & Derngate's acclaimed seasons of *Made in Northampton* work have included *Young America* (Northampton and National Theatre, London) and *End of the Rainbow* (Northampton and West End). Productions for 2015 included Shakespeare's *King John* and world premieres of Arthur Miller's *The Hook* (in a co-production with Liverpool Everyman & Playhouse) and Aldous Huxley's *Brave New World*.

The theatre also runs a wide-ranging *Get Involved* participatory programme which reached over 23,000 people last year, through projects in schools, within the community and at the theatre.

royalandderngate.co.uk | 01604 624811

THE MASSIVE TRAGEDY OF MADAME BOVARY

Gustave Flaubert

adapted by John Nicholson & Javier Marzan

A Note from the Authors

This play was written in response to a research period in Liverpool in December 2014 where we played with the framing device that a group of players are exploring how best to do justice to *Madame Bovary* in their stage adaptation. In the resulting *The Massive Tragedy of Madame Bovary*, the actors play meta-versions of themselves (using their own names) as well as all the significant characters from Flaubert's original novel. During the research we explored the pendulum swing between comedy and tragedy and how, when juxtaposed, comedy can expose tragedy and tragedy can expose comedy.

Special thanks go to Tom Morris, Mick Barnfather, Madeleine Worrall, Tim Dalling, Anthony Almeida and the director of the show's premiere, Gemma Bodinetz, who were all part of this research, and also to the show's original cast members, Jonathan Holmes and Emma Fielding, who provided additional invaluable input during rehearsals.

Characters

ACTOR 1, *Emma*
ACTOR 2, *Jonathan*
ACTOR 3, *John*
ACTOR 4, *Javier*
BLIND MAN
HIPPOLYTE
TUVACHE
HOMAIS
MME CODOUX
CHARLES BOVARY
JUSTIN
BAILIFF
EMMA'S MOTHER
MOTHER SUPERIOR
SISTER, *a nun*
ROAULT
MOTHER
MARCHIONESS
VISCOUNT
FOOTMAN
LÉON
LHEUREUX
COACH DRIVER
CURÉ
ROBERT
RODOLPHE
GIRARD
CAVINET
BEADLE
CAB DRIVER
FARMHANDS

Note on Text

The play is written for four actors. The actors use their own names (and play versions of themselves) when they talk directly to the audience. The cast names used in the original production have been used in this script.

In the original production, Actor 4 was a Spanish actor and some of the dialogue was written accordingly and may need to be adjusted in future productions.

The advised casting works as follows:

ACTOR 1 (Emma): Emma Bovary, Mme Codoux

ACTOR 2 (Jonathan): Blind man, Bailiff, Marchioness, Homais, Sister, Farmhand, Footman, Hippolyte, Justin, Lheureux, Curé, Girard, Beadle

ACTOR 3 (John): Charles Bovary, Emma's Mother, Mother Superior, Cab Driver, Robert

ACTOR 4 (Javier): Léon, Rodolphe, Roault, Dr Cavinet, Viscount

This text went to press before the end of rehearsals and so may differ slightly from the play as performed.

ACT ONE

Scene One

JAVIER *and* JOHN *sitting on a dog cart.* JAVIER *is singing 'One Thousand Green Bottles' in Spanish at the top of his voice.*

JOHN. Have you any idea how much the quality of my life would improve if you learnt another song?

JAVIER. No, it's a total mystery to me what goes on inside your head.

JOHN. What does that sign say?

JAVIER. 'Yonville, one kilometre.' This contract is going to change our lives. Yonville today, Paris tomorrow!

JOHN. Paris might not be all it's cracked up to be, you know.

JAVIER. What are you talking about? The most exciting city in the world?

JOHN. Says the man who's never been there.

JAVIER. I might not have been there physically, but I've walked down the Champs-Élysées…

JOHN. No you haven't…

JAVIER. I've wandered through the Louvre…

JOHN. We've been through this.

JAVIER. I'm basically a Parisian.

JOHN. You're basically… not. Let's just focus on not screwing this one up, shall we?

JAVIER. Relax. They've got the rats, we've got the remedy. What can go wrong?

The BLIND MAN *suddenly appears through the trapdoor in front of them. Sound of a horse rearing up.*

JOHN. Whoa! Where did he come from?

JAVIER. What are you doing in the middle of the road, man!? Are you blind or what?

BLIND MAN. Yes, I'm a blind troubadour, en route to Yonville.

JAVIER. Ha. What a coincidence. So are we.

BLIND MAN. Damn. Three blind troubadours in one town. That's gonna be overkill.

JAVIER. No, no. We're vermin controllers.

BLIND MAN. How do you see the rats?

JOHN. And we're not blind either. Can we offer you a lift?

BLIND MAN. Can you describe the vehicle?

JAVIER. Well, the seat's about four feet off the ground with a step up on the front axle.

The BLIND MAN *leaps up beside them.*

BLIND MAN. Merci.

The cart continues.

JOHN. What's your name, blind man?

BLIND MAN. Yes.

JAVIER. What songs do you know?

The BLIND MAN *starts to sing 'One Thousand Green Bottles'.* EMMA *writes 'Yonville' on the set.*

BLIND MAN.
Une centaine de bouteilles vertes accroché au mur,
Une centaine de bouteilles vertes accroché au mur,
Et si une bouteille verte devraient tomber
accidentellement...

Scene Two

Yonville Town Square.

JOHN. There we go, sir.

BLIND MAN. Good luck murdering the rats.

JOHN. And good luck murdering those songs! Sorry. Just a joke.

BLIND MAN. Don't apologise. A propensity for witticism is clearly in your nature and we can't escape that. Just as we can't escape our destiny.

He exits.

JOHN. What a load of baloney. Come on, let's get Bathsheba stabled.

They jump down and turn the cart around.

Come on, girl, around you go. This way – come on. Right, you fetch her some water, I'll check us in.

JAVIER *draws a tap and fills the bucket that* JOHN *hands to him.*

Well, this is it – The Golden Lion. We've stayed in worse places, I suppose.

He walks to the door and knocks.

Hello. Hello?

JAVIER. Ladies and gentlemen, just to address any confusion, the characters that John and I are currently playing are just a framing device.

JOHN. What are you doing?

JAVIER. Just give me a moment. Whenever we get to this point in the show, I've noticed quite a few confused faces.

JONATHAN. What's going on?

JOHN. Nothing.

JAVIER. Jonathan, would you or would you not agree that a little explanation of John's framing-device idea at this point wouldn't go amiss?

JONATHAN. Umm...

JAVIER. I mean, the plot of *Madame Bovary* is murky enough in the public consciousness and then on top of that we're introducing these rat-catchers who aren't even in the original...

JOHN. It's fine. The audience catch up eventually.

JAVIER. Exactly. 'Eventually.' I mean, if you'd adapted something more familiar like *Lady Chastity's Lover*, for example...

JOHN. *Lady* Chatterley's *Lover*.

JAVIER. I'm sure I wouldn't need to be saying any of this. Cha-tities.

JOHN. Chatterley.

JAVIER. Chattery.

JOHN. Leave it.

JAVIER. Well, you say potato, I say patatas con chorizo.

EMMA. What's going on? Why is he talking about tapas?

JAVIER. Bloody hell, this is turning into a much bigger deal than it needs to be.

JOHN. Yes it is.

JAVIER. Look, I just thought it'd be useful to briefly outline what's going on. Cos, let's be honest, the book is not that well known.

EMMA. Hang on. Not that well known? *Madame Bovary*?

JAVIER. Well, I suspect people will have heard of the title...

JONATHAN. And that she had some affairs.

EMMA. Can we please not reduce it to that!

JONATHAN. That's not me. Blame the people I've asked.

EMMA. What, people with penises?

JONATHAN. Mainly.

JOHN. Right, ladies and gentlemen, can we just get a quick show of hands if you've read *Madame Bovary*? Thank you. So, all *you* need to know is that the characters you've seen so far simply provide a jumping-off point into the novel. For the rest of you, we're beginning at the end of the novel. But that will become obvious. Let's continue.

JAVIER. John, come on. That's hardly a useful plot summary. Look at this guy – he looks even more confused now. You, madame, who hasn't got a penis I presume, you could help him out a bit – what's your favourite bit?

EMMA. No wait, stop! Favourite bit?

JAVIER. Okay, dramatic apogee.

EMMA. No! You can't reduce a book like this to a list of highlights.

This is an intimate study of a woman striving to have some control over her destiny in a heavily patriarchal society...

JONATHAN. *Heavily* patriarchal.

EMMA. Who eventually commits suicide.

JONATHAN. Shouldn't have had to.

JAVIER. That's a bit of a spoiler, Emma.

EMMA. Except she doesn't die in this adaptation.

JOHN. Even more of a spoiler!!

EMMA. My point is, you can't be so reductive with this book.

JONATHAN. No. It's an intimate study of a highly complex woman. And I'm not saying *all* women are complex. Some are surprisingly straightforward.

EMMA. Jonathan, I know you're trying really hard these days to support gender equality, but it's actually really annoying.

JAVIER. And not as attractive to women as you think either.
That's just from observing you in the bar after the shows.

JONATHAN. Shall we move on?

JAVIER. Yes, I think people have got the gist of the story now.

EMMA. What – that Madame Bovary is some French tart who
had some affairs and then committed suicide?

JOHN. I think we're trying to avoid reducing it to that, Emma.

JONATHAN. And anyway, it's not what happens.

EMMA. Well, it is.

JONATHAN. Yeah. But she's not a tart.

EMMA. I never said she was!

JAVIER.…well…

JONATHAN. If I might be permitted to quote Flaubert
himself… it's a story about nothing.

JOHN. Oh, nice one, Jonathan. I bet everyone's dying to see it
now.

JAVIER. I think we should begin.

EMMA. No, wait. I really must just clear this one up too.
Flaubert didn't *mean* nothing. He meant he was being honest
about people's lives – dissatisfaction, the desire to escape,
the tendency to spend more time dreaming about the lifestyle
we'd like than living the one we've actually got.

JONATHAN. I can relate to that.

EMMA. I mean, if I was in Emma's situation, I might have
totally lost the plot too.

JONATHAN. Who wouldn't?

EMMA. No, I'm not saying *everyone* would, Jonathan.

JONATHAN. Just women?

EMMA. No! Not just women. Blimey!

JOHN. Jonathan, go and put your wooden leg on.

Everyone moves towards starting positions.

Emma, just for the record, that was my understanding of the novel too.

JAVIER. Yonville, Northern France. 1850… something.

Scene Three

Yonville Town Square. The sound of horses, children, hubbub.
JONATHAN *attaches a wooden leg to his knee.*

HIPPOLYTE. Afternoon, gentlemen, my name is Hippolyte, welcome to The Golden Lion. Will you get away! Sorry, not you, the rats. I've just beeswaxed my leg – it's like catnip for them. Can I help you with your bags?

JOHN. No! Sorry – it's highly technical equipment. Very kind of you to offer though. We actually need to see the mayor. Any idea where we'll find him?

HIPPOLYTE. Monsieur Tuvache? Try the Town Hall. Across the square.

JAVIER. Merci.

JAVIER *and* JOHN *cross to a door and knock.* JONATHAN *has had to do a lightning-fast quick-change.*

TUVACHE. Entre.

JOHN. Mr Tuvache?

TUVACHE. Ah, ha! Are you the rat-catchers?

JOHN. Vermin termination executives.

TUVACHE. Well, you say potatoes, I say pommes de terre. You've seen the rats, then?

JAVIER. Hard to ignore.

TUVACHE. Exactly. But everyone does – they barely get a mention. Everyone's far more focused on the affairs of Madame Bovary.

JOHN. Who?

TUVACHE. You'll find out. I want to put this town back on the map. 'Monsieur Tuvache, the saviour of Yonville!' people will cry. So, rat-free in three days according to this revolutionary new formula of yours?

JAVIER. That's our promise.

TUVACHE. I'll hold you to it. As agreed, half the money upfront, the remainder on completion. Here.

JOHN. Thank you. We'll go and unpack.

Scene Four

Hotel room.

JAVIER. Six thousand francs! This is more money than I've ever held! Six thousand francs! Paris, here we come.

JOHN. As long as our secret ingredients don't let us down...

He opens the suitcase and starts unpacking.

Camembert, Brie, Emmental, Roquefort, Boursin, Cheddar...

JAVIER. The rats in France won't go for that.

JOHN. Hang on, where's the arsenic?

JAVIER. What?

JOHN. The arsenic?

JAVIER. I thought you packed it.

JOHN. Me!? I'm on cheese! You're on arsenic!

JAVIER. Okay. Let's focus on the positive here.

JOHN. The positive?!

JAVIER. Obviously this was meant to happen.

JOHN. What!?

JAVIER. In this universe. In another universe, I didn't forget it.

JOHN. You'd better get to a pharmacy. And quick.

JAVIER. Why? I feel fine.

JOHN. And buy up all the arsenic you can get your hands on!

JAVIER. And reveal our most important secret ingredient?

JOHN. So don't tell them what it's for!

JAVIER. So who shall I say I am?

JOHN. I don't know. Think of something!

Scene Five

The pharmacy.

HOMAIS. Will that be all, Madame Codoux?

MME CODOUX. And a do-it-yourself bloodletting kit.

HOMAIS. Ah. Those have been discontinued – one or two accidents. I suggest a visit to Dr Bovary.

MME CODOUX. Really? After that hatchet job he did on Hippolyte's foot?

HOMAIS. Well, admittedly things could have turned out better there.

MME CODOUX. Yeah, he could still have two legs. I'm not one to gossip but I've had it from a reliable source that Charles Bovary only scraped through medical school. And as for that wife of his – carrying on like a Parisian socialite. I've said it before and I'll say it again – she's bleeding him dry.

HOMAIS. I'd say that's a private matter between Madame
    Bovary and her husband.

MME CODOUX. Yeah, if he's aware of her spending. Cos let's
    face it, he hasn't noticed the men.

HOMAIS. Madame Codoux!

MME CODOUX. First Rodolphe then Léon. Could be any one
    of us next.

    JAVIER *enters*.

HOMAIS. Bonjour, monsieur. How can I help?

JAVIER. I'm a gardener.

MME CODOUX. I thought you were a rat-catcher.

JAVIER. I see news travels fast around here.

HOMAIS. Nothing gets by Madame Codoux.

MME CODOUX. And you've got a secret formula, I hear.

HOMAIS. I'd keep the ingredients of that well under wraps if I
    were you. So, what can I get you?

JAVIER. I'll come back later.

HOMAIS. Well, we're about to close up for the weekend, so if
    it's anything urgent.

JAVIER. Um… Right. Some of that please.

HOMAIS. Wart powder?

MME CODOUX. Is that one of the ingredients?

JAVIER. Might be.

HOMAIS. Anything else?

JAVIER. Yes. One of every item on that shelf, and that shelf.
    And some hair wax, sink unblock, potassium, washing
    powder… (*Under his breath.*) arsenic.

HOMAIS. Sorry, didn't catch that last one.

JAVIER (*with cough*). Arsenic.

HOMAIS. Again?

MME CODOUX. Arsenic! He wants arsenic!

HOMAIS. Right. How much are you after?

JAVIER (*under his breath*). How much have you got?

HOMAIS. Again?

MME CODOUX. How much have you got!?

HOMAIS. A full jar, I believe.

JAVIER (*under his breath*). I'll take the lot.

HOMAIS. And once more?

MME CODOUX. He wants to buy all the arsenic in the shop!
What are you, deaf?

HOMAIS. Right. Justin, hand me the cabinet keys, will you?

Keys come through a hole in the back wall. HOMAIS
unlocks the cabinet. CHARLES *enters.*

CHARLES (*breathless*). Homais. It's me, Charles Bovary.

JAVIER. I'm a gardener!

CHARLES. Have you seen my wife, Madame Bovary?

HOMAIS. Not since this morning. Anything I can do, Charles?
Bovary.

CHARLES. I don't think so. Not this time.

He rushes out.

MME CODOUX. Well, well.

JUSTIN (*voice-over*). What's happened?

HOMAIS. Nothing to concern you, Justin. Stay out of sight. Dr
Bovary was just looking for his wife, Madame Bovary.

MME CODOUX. The poor boy's besotted with her. Gets a
perk-on every time he sees her.

JUSTIN (*voice-over*). No I don't!

HOMAIS. Madame Codoux, that's enough! There's your arsenic, monsieur. Where are you staying?

MME CODOUX. The Golden Lion – that's where they're staying. There's two of them.

HOMAIS. We'll get the rest of your order packed into some crates.

JAVIER. Actually, cancel the rest of the order. I'm a gardener!

JAVIER *exits*. MME CODOUX *follows after him*.

MME CODOUX. What do you use as bait? Cheese, is it? What kind of cheese?

JAVIER. Leave me alone, old woman!

MME CODOUX. Ooh. Sexist.

CHARLES *enters*.

CHARLES. Homais!

HOMAIS. Charles Bovary?

CHARLES. Yes. Charles Bovary.

HOMAIS. What's going on now, Charles Bovary?

CHARLES. I need your help! You have to hide me.

HOMAIS. Follow me, Charles Bovary. You can go through to the back. (*Switches to* BAILIFF.)

BAILIFF. Monsieur Bovary? As a bailiff granted with a warrant to enter your house, I have a warrant to enter your house and seize items of capital against unpaid debts.

CHARLES. No! Please, you can't do this to me. I have a wife and daughter to support.

BAILIFF. Either you hand over the keys or we break the door down.

CHARLES *exits with the* BAILIFF.

CHARLES (*off*). My wife is Madame Bovary and my five-year-old daughter is Berthe Bovary. Please...!

HOMAIS. Charles? (*Then notices a packet of pills*.) Justin, I'll be back in a minute, Mme Codoux has forgotten her amphetamines again. Lock the door behind me, will you?

JUSTIN (*voice-over*). I'll need the keys.

HOMAIS. Good point. There you go.

HOMAIS *exits*.

Scene Six

JAVIER. So, the scene is set. The bailiff has gone off with Charles to repossess his possessions. Homais is running around with amphetamines, Justin is closing up the apothecary. And night is falling. Enter Madame Bovary.

He pulls out a copy of the book and reads.

'*She stood in a daze. Conscious of herself only through the throbbing of her arteries, the sound of which seemed to fill the countryside. The earth beneath her feet was more yielding than the sea. Memories, came rushing forth like a thousand explosions. Her father, her mother, the room she grew up in. Her attempts that day to alleviate the crippling debts she had amounted seemed like a distant memory now. Although everyone knew. Everyone that is, apart from Charles, who loved her so much that he was unable to see the truth. And in that respect, he had his part to play. In a sudden ecstasy of fearlessness, that made her almost joyous, she ran down the hill, crossed the cow-plank, the footpath, the alley, the market square, and reached the pharmacy.*'

Pharmacy.

EMMA. Justin. Open up. Quickly.

JUSTIN. Madame Bovary!? I'm afraid the pharmacy is closed.

EMMA. It's an emergency.

JUSTIN *opens the door.*

JUSTIN. The doctor was looking for you earlier. Did he find you? There were bailiffs...

EMMA (*fainting*). Oh God...

JUSTIN. Here? Sit down. I'll get you some water.

EMMA. No. I'm fine. I just need your keys to the cabinet.

JUSTIN. The cabinet? Why?

EMMA. Shhh. Don't worry. It's all going to be fine. Where are they? Where do you keep them? Tell me, Justin?

JUSTIN. They're in my pocket.

EMMA. This pocket?

JUSTIN. Yes.

EMMA. Thank you.

JUSTIN. If you tell me what it is you need...

She crosses to the cabinet and opens it.

EMMA. Where is it? Where's the arsenic!

JUSTIN. We sold it all this afternoon.

EMMA. No! Then perhaps I shall die of despair instead.

JUSTIN. Die?

EMMA. Who did you sell it to, Justin? Tell me!

JUSTIN. A Spaniard. He's boarding at The Golden Lion.

She rushes out. Dramatic transition.

Madame Bovary!

Scene Seven

The Golden Lion. JAVIER *and* JOHN *are sat.* HIPPOLYTE
brings drinks to the table.

JOHN. Well, did you get it?

JAVIER. The arsenic? Yes! All of it!

HIPPOLYTE. There we go, gentlemen.

JAVIER. Merci. Santé!

JOHN. Santé! So, you seem to get by pretty well on one leg,
    Hippolyte.

HIPPOLYTE. It wasn't strictly Dr Bovary's fault – what
    happened to me. I'm not going to hold it against him.

JAVIER. The leg?

HIPPOLYTE. The responsibility.

JOHN. So what happened?

HIPPOLYTE. To the leg? Dunno. I guess they just binned it.

JOHN. No. I mean what went wrong?

    EMMA *bursts in.*

HIPPOLYTE. Madame Bovary!

EMMA. Are you the Spaniard?

JAVIER. Yes. Well, there's more of us in Spain.

EMMA. I need to talk to you. Alone.

    JOHN *moves away.*

    The arsenic you bought today. I need some. I don't have
    money but you can take this ring.

JAVIER. Now, wait a minute.

EMMA. We have a problem with rats.

JAVIER. Then you've come to the right people.

EMMA. Excuse me?

JAVIER. My friend and I are vermin termination executives.

EMMA. What?

JAVIER. We kill rats.

EMMA. Oh. Well, it's actually for a taxidermy project. It's a useful preserving agent.

JAVIER. Is that so?

EMMA. And you've bought up the pharmacy's full supply.

JAVIER. What are you stuffing?

EMMA. I'm sorry?

JAVIER. I was wondering what the animal in question was.

EMMA. A cat. All right? I'm stuffing the family cat.

JAVIER. Sounds urgent.

EMMA. Yes! It is! Will you just help me out and give me the damned arsenic!?

JAVIER. Madame Bovary, I'm only reading between the lines here, but if you ingest arsenic, it will take two days of violent suffering before you die.

EMMA. You know nothing about me!

JAVIER. No. Only that I suspect you want to escape from this life.

EMMA. You're wrong. You couldn't possibly understand.

JAVIER. I might want to escape too.

EMMA. From this life?

JAVIER. Well, from this provincial life.

EMMA. Are you telling me you want to move house!?

JAVIER. Sí. To Paris.

EMMA (*the dream*). Paris!?

JAVIER. Have you been?

EMMA. Yes. I mean, no. Not physically. But I've walked down the Champs-Élysées...

JAVIER. Me too.

EMMA. Really?

JAVIER. Not physically. But I've wandered through the Louvre...

EMMA. Me too. I've sat in cafés.

JAVIER. Me too. I've strolled along the Seine.

EMMA. Me too. I've whiled away afternoons in dress shops.

JAVIER. Me too.

EMMA. The uncertain promise of living there always hung in the future for me, like a golden fruit suspended beneath some fantastic bough.

JAVIER. You've taken the words right out of my mouth. But in a different order. And with different words.

EMMA. But the dream became a dark corridor with a bolted door.

JAVIER. Oh right.

EMMA. It's easy for you. You're free. You'll go to Paris.

JAVIER. Now you're presuming to know *me*.

EMMA. You're a man. That's all I need to know. My husband! He's heading this way across the square.

JAVIER. Follow me. You can head up the back stairs.

JOHN. What's going on?

JAVIER. I'll be right behind you.

JOHN. Where's she off to?

JAVIER. My room.

JOHN. Rock on.

JAVIER. It's not like that! You know when I said there was a reason I forgot the arsenic – well, this is it.

JOHN. To have an affair with a married woman?

JAVIER. No. To save her!

Scene Eight

Transition to a bedroom in the inn.

JAVIER. Here, Emma, drink this. Why don't you come and sit down?

EMMA. Do you know how much of my life I've spent looking out of windows?

JAVIER. About half?

EMMA. About half.

JAVIER. Because they feel like a portal to another life?

EMMA. How do you know these things about me!?

JAVIER. I don't. I'm just quite in to imagery. And women. You seem like you've been on quite a journey today.

EMMA. There were people I hoped could help me.

JAVIER. Like your lover, Rodolphe?

EMMA. Right – what's going on here?

JAVIER. That's just from gossip.

EMMA. This insipid town! This insipid life!

JAVIER. Things can change.

EMMA. Oh, can they? Really!? How? Everyone else always thinks they know best, don't they.

JAVIER. And how is ingesting arsenic a solution?

EMMA. Who the hell are you to tell me it isn't?

JAVIER. Well, like I say, I'm a vermin termination executive.

EMMA. I don't believe this.

JAVIER. I am. (*Beat.*) Nobody wants you to die.

EMMA. You don't get it, do you. This isn't about anyone else. It's about me! I don't want to be unhappy any more!

JAVIER *pours her another drink.*

JAVIER. What's your first memory?

EMMA. What?

JAVIER. What's the first thing you remember?

EMMA. What are you talking about?

JAVIER. Tell me.

EMMA. No. Fuck off.

JAVIER. I remember my dad lassoing me.

EMMA. –

JAVIER. He used to make me run away from him and then he would try to catch me with a rope.

EMMA. Why?

JAVIER. For fun.

EMMA. And was it?

JAVIER. Of course it was. Imagine it.

Pause. JAVIER *takes a bite of an apple* (*a prop that distinguishes his character*).

EMMA. I remember the apple harvest.

Scene Nine

First one apple, then dozens tumble from a trapdoor in the back wall. FARMHANDS *collect them.* JOHN *becomes an apple tree, then* EMMA'S MOTHER, *who* EMMA *sings with.*

EMMA. My mother holding me up to the lower branches to pick fruit as she sang. The light, the perfume, the hum of the afternoon. The way she tried to hide the roughness of her hands. The way my father made us laugh. Until she became ill.

'If I had a lake to swim in,
And a blackbird to sing,
And woods to walk in,
And a diamond ring,
And a fireplace to sit by,
And a garden with a view,
It would all mean nothing,
If I didn't have you.'

EMMA'S MOTHER *has departed.*

JAVIER. When did she die?

EMMA. I'd been sent to a convent. My parents wanted me educated.

EMMA *prays.* MOTHER SUPERIOR *enters.*

Scene Ten

MOTHER SUPERIOR. Emma Roault?

EMMA. Mother Superior.

MOTHER SUPERIOR. Your eagerness in some aspects of life here has not gone unnoticed. But if you wish to take the veil, the sacrifice is absolute. You must surrender desire. God will grant you the strength.

SISTER enters, beckons to MOTHER SUPERIOR.

SISTER. Mother?

MOTHER SUPERIOR. What is it?

SISTER. I found this book in her drawer. I can't bring myself to recount the details, but it involved an Italian sailor.

MOTHER SUPERIOR. Is this true, Emma?

EMMA. You'd better ask her. I haven't read it yet.

MOTHER SUPERIOR. But you admit it belongs to you?

EMMA. Yes.

SISTER. And these fashion magazines. And this.

MOTHER SUPERIOR. What's this?

SISTER. A drawing of the Lord chopping wood. Without a shirt on.

EMMA. What makes you think it's Jesus?

MOTHER SUPERIOR. The halo is a bit of a giveaway, Emma.

Snap lighting change.

ROAULT. Emma?

EMMA. Father. What are you doing here?

ROAULT. –

EMMA. What is it?

ROAULT. Your mother is dead, Emma.

EMMA. But... your letters... I thought there was hope.

ROAULT. I had convinced myself there was. I've brought you her rosary.

EMMA. When is the funeral?

ROAULT. She was buried yesterday. Under her favourite apple tree.

Snap lighting change.

MOTHER SUPERIOR. Emma. The sacrifices to be made lie within your governance.

EMMA. Father, joy is discouraged in this place. They want to break me.

MOTHER SUPERIOR. What do you want for yourself, Emma?

EMMA. I want to be happy. Just that!

Scene Eleven

The farm begins to form around them.

ROAULT. Emma, I'm glad you're coming home – it's far too
quiet without you.

EMMA *wanders, savouring being home. We pass through
the seasons. In the montage she changes from girl to young
woman, dressed accordingly. She sits in a chair, content. She
flicks through a magazine.*

EMMA (*voice-over*). 'The emerging Parisian woman will be
strong-minded, strong-hearted and strong-souled. Strength
and beauty must go together...' 'The cage crinoline – a
flexible steel framework joined by tapes or string and having
no covering fabric – are set to become this season's most
sought-after garment...'

Her father falls from a table.

ROAULT. Agghh!

EMMA. Father? Father!? Help!

She runs to him.

What happened?

ROAULT. I fell from the apple tree.

EMMA. Help! Can you move?

ROAULT. It's my leg. Get the axe. Chop it off.

FARMHANDS *rush in.* ROAULT *is stretchered to a bed.*

EMMA. That's how I met Charles. He arrived on his horse that
afternoon.

Scene Twelve

EMMA. A black mare, as I remember.

A riding crop is thrown on stage.

I greeted him at the door and we went straight up to see my father.

ROAULT. Are you the doctor?

CHARLES. Yes.

ROAULT. I don't need a doctor.

EMMA. He does. He's been drinking.

ROAULT. No I haven't. Bring me more brandy.

CHARLES. Let's take a look. Ah. This seems pretty straightforward to deal with.

EMMA. You must be very skilled.

CHARLES. No.

EMMA. No?

CHARLES. I mean, it's a simple fracture. I'll make up a splint.

EMMA *exits to another room and nervously busies herself.* CHARLES *appears and watches her. She senses him and turns.*

EMMA. Is there something you need?

CHARLES. My riding crop.

EMMA. Your riding crop? Why?

CHARLES. For my horse. It makes it speed up.

EMMA. Oh, I see. You've finished with my father, then?

CHARLES. Yes. I mean no. I'll need to return to check up on him.

EMMA. Good. I mean here. For your journey back.

She hands him a glass. She takes his hat. There is confusion. Then:

CHARLES. Thank you. I should look for my crop.

They both look around the room without moving. Their eyes keep meeting. Then:

EMMA. I see it.

CHARLES. Ah, yes. How did it get all the way over there?

EMMA. You must have tossed it aside when you arrived. With some force.

CHARLES. How careless.

EMMA. It's the heat. Sometimes when I'm reading I just throw the book aside and... I'll fetch it.

CHARLES. No, I can.

Their hands touch as they both reach for the crop at the same time.

EMMA. When will you return? Soon?

CHARLES. In the morning?

EMMA. Come for breakfast. If you like.

CHARLES. Very well. Where's the door?

EMMA. I don't know. There.

They make towards the door, CHARLES *drops his crop again.*

I'll fetch it.

CHARLES. No, I can. Until tomorrow.

Sound of a horse leaving.

EMMA. The only men I had known up to this point were farm workers. Charles was from a different world. My naive imagination refracted his every action into gallantry, his every sentence into perceptiveness.

Scene Thirteen

CHARLES *appears*.

CHARLES. Forgive me. I'm a little early.

EMMA. Yes. It's still dark.

CHARLES. I'll wait in the barn.

EMMA. No, please, come in. Can I get you a drink? Coffee? Or a brandy? I'll get both.

CHARLES. How's your father?

EMMA. He seems settled.

CHARLES. My wife died.

EMMA. Last night!?

CHARLES. No, no. Four months ago.

EMMA. Goodness. How have you managed to cope?

CHARLES. My mother moved in and took over the accounts.

EMMA. Oh.

CHARLES. But she needn't stay living with us. Me! I mean, it's a temporary arrangement – I plan to get rid of her. Not kill her, just kick her out. Move her out. Back to her own house.

EMMA *hands him a drink and knocks hers back*.

EMMA. Woo! Quite strong, isn't it.

She licks the glass.

CHARLES. This is a cracking kitchen.

EMMA. Would you like to see my bedroom?

CHARLES. Um...

EMMA. I've got a lot of books. I've read most of them. Or I could do some cooking. Shall I cook a roast?

CHARLES. Do you have eggs?

EMMA. No, but we have ducks. I mean, we have ducks that lay eggs. I'll check.

EMMA *draws a duck, removes an egg from a flap in the back wall, cracks it into a bowl and beats it.*

Poached or boiled?

CHARLES. Either. Both.

EMMA. Right. I'll do my best. The cock should crow soon.

Sound of a cock crowing.

CHARLES. Ah. Like cock work.

EMMA. Excuse me?

CHARLES. I was comparing the punctuality of your cock to a clock.

EMMA. That's so clever. I could never play with words like that.

CHARLES. Do you like spoonerisms?

EMMA. Things like spoons?

CHARLES. No, no. It's when you change words around. For example: it is kisstomary to cuss the bride.

EMMA. Is it?

CHARLES. No. It's customary to kiss the bride but I changed it.

EMMA. Look at this hat. I won it for a poem at my convent.

CHARLES. What was the poem about?

EMMA. Passion.

CHARLES. I went to a prep school. Probably quite different to a convent.

EMMA. I would imagine so.

CHARLES. What was it like?

EMMA. Part of it enthralled me. Sometimes I would invent sins so I could stay longer in the confession box. But I left. Soon after my mother died.

CHARLES. Your father mentioned her last night.

EMMA. He used to say that his heart felt like a lump of dead wood after she'd gone.

CHARLES. He's still saying it. It can't have been easy.

EMMA. No. I missed her until it felt like I had nothing left to feel. But *now* I want to feel. I want to feel life. I want to inhale it. I want to stand in the heart of a storm and be consumed by its force. I want to… It sounds like Father's awake.

ROAULT *is heard offstage, loudly retching.*

He kept drinking last night. To reduce the pain.

EMMA *exits, taking him a bedpan. More retching.* CHARLES *gets his finger stuck in a teacup.* EMMA *enters, offers coffee, realises his predicament and fetches a sledgehammer. She taps the handle to break it. It's an intimate moment.*

CHARLES. Thank you.

He collects the broken pieces and places them in the cup. His hand ends up on EMMA's *breast.* ROAULT *appears. He stares at* CHARLES.

Mr Roault! I've just come to check up on you.

ROAULT. It appears that I should be checking on you. Why are you smashing up the crockery, Emma?

CHARLES. It was my fault. My finger got stuck.

EMMA. Our crockery is far too small for a soldier like Charles.

Pause.

CHARLES. Well. I suppose I should go.

EMMA. But you will come again?

CHARLES. Yes. Definitely.

ROAULT. No need to. The leg's fine.

CHARLES. All the same, I think I should return.

ROAULT. Look at me. I'm fine.

CHARLES. Then I shall return…

EMMA. For your payment.

CHARLES. Exactly.

ROAULT. No need. I can settle up now.

EMMA. No!

CHARLES (*loudly*). No. I don't want to trouble you. I really should be going.

ROAULT. Won't take a minute.

CHARLES. I shall return soon.

EMMA. Yes. Hurry. Until next time.

ROAULT. Do you want it in notes or coins?

CHARLES. Goodbye.

And he's gone.

ROAULT. I've got it right here. Where did he go? (*Following after him.*) Doctor! Doctor!

JAVIER reappears in his rat-catcher outfit.

EMMA. Even after he'd been paid, Charles insisted that he should regularly check up on my father. I had imagined this man for so long – this man I knew from every romantic novel I'd ever read. I seduced myself with the imprint I forced upon him. And in my fiction I was Joan of Arc; beautiful and strong.

Scene Fourteen

CHARLES *arrives at the farm on his horse. Actors are creating a farm/animals with the furniture. His request is drowned out by 'moos' 'oinks' and 'quacks'.*

ROAULT. Monsieur Bovary – this is getting ridiculous, look at me. I've even taken up tap-dancing classes.

CHARLES. Yes. The thing is, I want to ask you something.

ROAULT. Go ahead, I'm all ears.

CHARLES. It's about your –

Moooo!

–ter.

ROAULT. My what?

CHARLES. Your –

Moooo!

–ter

ROAULT. No. Again?

CHARLES. Monsieur. I am in –

Quack!

– with your –

Woof!

–ter

ROAULT. You'll have to be clearer.

CHARLES. I would like to –

Quack!

– for your –

Woof!

–ter's –

Baaaaa!

– in –

Mooo!

–age.

ROAULT. You'd like to quack for my woofter's baaaa in moo-rage?

CHARLES. Will you all shut up! I'd like to ask for your daughter's hand in marriage.

ROAULT. Ahh! My good man, why didn't you say? You were talking in riddles! You go and stand in that field over there. If the lass says yes, I'll throw open the shutters and you'll have your answer.

CHARLES. Right. The field just there?

ROAULT. No, that's very marshy. Wait up behind the stream.

CHARLES. Near those poplars?

ROAULT. No, there's a bull in that field.

CHARLES. The field to the left?

ROAULT. Freshly planted.

CHARLES. Behind that?

ROAULT. That's my neighbour's. You'll probably get a bullet in your arse.

CHARLES. Well, where shall I wait then!?

ROAULT. In with the sheep. You'll have a clear view of the house from there.

CHARLES *stands in the rain. Sound of sheep. We wait. And wait. With a flourish, the shutters burst open. The rain stops. The sun comes out.* EMMA *appears in a wedding dress.*

Scene Fifteen

CHARLES *approaches* EMMA. *Candles are lit.*

CHARLES. You look beautiful.

EMMA. Don't let go of my hand.

CHARLES. I'm not going to. Are you happy?

EMMA. How could I not be happy? It's my wedding day.

We fade to a shadow of a four-poster bed.

Scene Sixteen

CHARLES *undresses.* EMMA *throws herself onto the bed in various positions.* CHARLES *continues with his routine. Image fades.* EMMA *appears downstage.*

EMMA. I thought the world would open up. I thought everything would look different.

She blows out a candle. It's instantly morning. CHARLES *enters.*

CHARLES. Don't you think the world looks different? I've never felt this way. Ever.

EMMA. That's wonderful.

CHARLES. You are more wonderful than I could have ever dreamed of, Emma Bovary.

EMMA. We'll make it work, won't we, Charles? Everything is going to change.

CHARLES. Everything *has* changed. Hasn't it?

EMMA. Of course it has. Let's try again. Rip this dress off me. Push me up against the wall. Tell me how much you want me. Do it, Charles!

CHARLES (*amused/bemused*). Why?

EMMA. Forget it.

CHARLES. Right. I think we're expected for the wedding breakfast. I'm starving, aren't you? There'll be croissants, brioche, pain au chocolat, baguettes, French toast. Everything you could desire.

Yonville. EMMA *turns on a radio which is chalked up on the wall and 'Non, je ne regrette rien' plays. She starts to beat eggs. She decides to throw out everything in the house. She moves the set, creating their house.* CHARLES's MOTHER *enters. 'La Maison de Bovary' is chalked up on the wall.*

Scene Seventeen

MOTHER. What's she doing, Charles?

CHARLES. She's homemaking, Mother.

MOTHER. Are you sure about that? Do you think you've made the right decision?

CHARLES. Mother, please! I love her.

MOTHER. You'd have to.

CHARLES. What's that supposed to mean?

MOTHER. What advice can I give you? I mean, I'm *only* your mother.

CHARLES. I'm not asking for advice. I'm asking for your blessing.

EMMA. Charles, what's this?

MOTHER. His first wife's wedding bouquet.

EMMA. Oh. Nice.

She drops it in the bin. MOTHER *exits in reaction.*
CHARLES *starts to run after her.*

CHARLES. Mother. Mother.

Then turns back to EMMA.

Listen, I'd better get going.

EMMA. Charles, no. Can't you stay?

CHARLES. I'm afraid I have an abscess of the mouth awaiting my attendance. So what might you get up to today?

EMMA. I have no idea.

CHARLES. Painting?

EMMA. The house?

CHARLES (*imagines she is joking*). No. A watercolour? It's just a suggestion.

EMMA. No. It's a good suggestion.

CHARLES. Good. I love you so much. See you for supper.

CHARLES *exits with a kiss.* EMMA *opens imaginary doors. A wind picks up. She stands in the middle of a storm. The storm subsides. She sits for supper with* CHARLES. *The clock ticks.*

Scene Eighteen

CHARLES. Christ, I love peas.

EMMA. Shall we make love in the garden tonight?

> CHARLES *finds this hilarious and presumes it's a joke.*
> *Then...*

CHARLES. Looks like Madame Belen de Français is heading
for consumption.

EMMA. Charles!

CHARLES. I'm sorry, darling. How was your day?

EMMA. Insipid.

CHARLES. Insipid...? (*Trying to remember the meaning of the*
word.)

EMMA. Dull, bland, unexciting, lifeless, boring! Charles, we
never DO anything! Have you noticed? We've been married
a year now and we never DO anything. Nothing happens.
You deal with your patients. I go for walks and sit under the
watchful eye of your bloody mother.

CHARLES. Now, wait there a second, I almost forgot. This
arrived.

He produces a letter. EMMA *takes it. Reads it.*

EMMA. It's from the Marquis d'Andervilliers. It's an invitation
to a ball at his château!

CHARLES. In return for the abscess I lanced in his mouth last
month.

EMMA. Oh, Charles! This is it! How could you overlook such
a thing? This is the most exciting news I've ever received.

CHARLES. What about my marriage proposal?

EMMA. I shall need a new dress!

Scene Nineteen

The music of the ball begins. The room forms around her. A chandelier descends and becomes EMMA*'s huge dress.*

EMMA. I remember the chandeliers – like a starlit sky, iced champagne fountains, the marble statues as tall as trees, the exquisite linen, quails with feathers still on them, tropical fruits piled high on moss-covered tables and red lobsters like you'd never seen.

CHARLES. Emma, look at all this stuff; cigars, champagne, pineapples! It's all free! And you can go back for more!

MARCHIONESS. You two look a little lost.

CHARLES. Yes. What a ridiculously extravagant house.

MARCHIONESS. It's been in my family for five generations.

CHARLES. Right. I didn't realise you were... I'm Dr Bovary, and this is my wife.

MARCHIONESS. I know.

EMMA. It's a beautiful house you have, Marchioness.

MARCHIONESS. Perhaps you'd like to play billiards, Dr Bovary?

CHARLES. Love to. You rack 'em up.

MARCHIONESS. While I talk to your beautiful wife?

CHARLES. Oh right. Yes. I'll go and... rack 'em up then.

He wanders off.

MARCHIONESS. He bores you, doesn't he?

EMMA. No.

MARCHIONESS. My dear, he's your husband. A degree of tedium comes with the marriage certificate. Do you waltz?

EMMA. No.

MARCHIONESS. How delicious. Let me find someone to
initiate you. Who do you like the look of?

EMMA. Really, I'm...

MARCHIONESS. The Viscount? He'll do. Viscount!

VISCOUNT *approaches. He's incredibly debonair.*

This poor girl has no one to dance with.

VISCOUNT. Then would madame perhaps do me the honour?

MARCHIONESS. Yes, she would.

They dance. The VISCOUNT *circles her on a scooter.*
Bigger and bigger dishes appear in crosses behind her.
CHARLES *becomes mistaken for a waiter and ends up as*
one, despite his cries of 'Emma!' and proudly 'That's my
wife!' until...

EMMA. I can't breathe. I'm going to faint.

VISCOUNT. The lady's going to faint.

FOOTMAN. The lady's going to faint.

VISCOUNT. Break the windows!

FOOTMAN. Break the windows!

The FOOTMAN *smashes the windows.*

EMMA. Don't stop!

VISCOUNT. Are you sure?

EMMA. I've never been more sure of anything.

The dance continues.

Don't stop. Ever!

EMMA *continues to dance. But the ball drifts away until she*
is alone with only her memories of the night.

Scene Twenty

She plays notes on a miniature piano. CHARLES *writes a diary entry.*

CHARLES. '20th June 1856. It's hard to imagine what more a man could want in this life than the situation I have reached. I busy myself with work. Emma loves to... choose curtain fabric... walk... in fact she seems most content just looking out of the window. It's idyllic. Love is like... a perfectly warmed bowl of soup.'

EMMA *begins to dance with the piano.*

MOTHER. What's she doing now, Charles?

CHARLES. She's dancing with a piano, Mother. What does it look like?

MOTHER. It looks like she's losing the plot. You know she gave all the change in her purse to a blind beggar the other day.

CHARLES. That was generous.

MOTHER. Generous? She's never been generous. It was madness.

CHARLES. Are you saying there's madness in generosity?

MOTHER. No. I'm saying there's generosity in madness. She'll be eating mud next.

Scene Twenty-one

We're back in the hotel room.

JAVIER. Did you ever meet the Viscount again?

EMMA. No. It was the only time in my life that I'd felt truly happy. Just for a moment, to glimpse the life that I might have had the chance to lead. Then it vanished.

JAVIER. That's more than a lot of people might experience.

EMMA. Well I'm not 'a lot of other people', am I. (*Beat.*) I'm the way I am.

JAVIER. Or the way you choose to be.

EMMA. Oh really? It's just a choice, is it – the way we feel? Like a switch we can flick? Tell me, have you ever been unable to get out of bed in the morning? Not because you're tired. Not because you feel sick. But because you're scared that the voice screaming your worthlessness will strangle you. When you're too numb to even beg that the feeling will pass. Have you ever had that feeling?

JAVIER. No.

EMMA. You think I choose to feel that? I can be selfish. Yes, I can be profligate and deceitful and pleasure-seeking and self-obsessed. I know what people think of me. But if I can't feel alive…

MOTHER. All that girl needs is a change of air.

CHARLES. And that's what she's getting. We're moving.

CHARLES *picks up cases.*

MOTHER. Moving?

CHARLES. To Yonville. And by the way. She's pregnant.

EMMA. Pregnant? Are you sure?

CHARLES. Yes, my love. My examination has confirmed it.
    Are you happy?

EMMA. I'm... amazed.

CHARLES. It *is* amazing, isn't it? It's the most amazing news.

Scene Twenty-two

Scene change to The Golden Lion.

EMMA. That's when we came here – to Yonville. Charles had
    been appointed as the country doctor. We arrived late. It was
    raining and cold. Homais was waiting to greet us and they
    had prepared a meal for us downstairs in The Golden Lion. I
    went inside to dry my freezing feet by the fire as the bags
    were unpacked.

LÉON. Are you the doctor's wife?

EMMA. Yes.

They suddenly notice each other properly.

Who are you?

CHARLES *and* HOMAIS *enter laden with cases.*

HOMAIS. Well, don't get up and help will you, Léon! Oh,
    don't trouble yourself. I'll do it.

He brings wine to the table.

CHARLES (*pulling out a chair*). Come, Emma.

*She comes to the table but LÉON already has a chair for her.
HOMAIS pours wine.*

HOMAIS. Bon appétit. And a toast to our new arrivals!

They sit.

When will you be ready to receive patients, Charles?

CHARLES. In a few days, I hope.

EMMA. So. You're Léon.

LÉON. Yes. I lodge with Homais. For my sins.

CHARLES. How is the general health of the town?

HOMAIS. Could be better.

LÉON. Welcome to Yonville.

EMMA. Should I be excited?

CHARLES. I'm so excited.

LÉON. I wouldn't get too worked up.

HOMAIS. We had a bout of scrofula last year and the effects seem to be lingering.

EMMA. So what does this thrilling town have to offer?

LÉON. Very little.

CHARLES. I can't wait to explore.

EMMA. Come on, there must be something?

HOMAIS. We've quite a few cases of gout.

CHARLES. Fascinating.

LÉON. Do you like agricultural fairs?

EMMA. Just you try and keep me away.

HOMAIS. And some nasty cases of foot-rot.

CHARLES. Ah yes.

LÉON. We have some beautiful sunsets though.

CHARLES. In Tostes they seemed to spring up every day.

LÉON. You get a magnificent view from the hill up there.

HOMAIS. It's hardly surprising.

EMMA. Really? I love the sun.

HOMAIS. I find the stench of it overwhelming.

LÉON. Especially when it sets over the sea. Have you ever seen that?

HOMAIS. I saw a particularly putrid example last week, actually.

EMMA. Yes. It looks like it's setting the water alight.

CHARLES. Sounds disgusting.

LÉON. Or like butter melting onto a mirror.

HOMAIS. Not dissimilar to a maggot farm.

CHARLES. Maggots are remarkable. Do you like peas?

EMMA. That's inspired.

HOMAIS. Love them.

EMMA. I'd like to float into a sunset while playing the piano.

HOMAIS. But...

EMMA. Naked.

HOMAIS. ...dripping in butter.

CHARLES. I can see we're going to get on...

LÉON. Well...

HOMAIS. I've been working on some pharmaceutical remedies myself actually.

LÉON. I'd like to stand on a glacier and sing.

CHARLES. What for?

EMMA. What about?

HOMAIS. The Black Death.

LÉON. Love.

CHARLES. Have you come across any cases of the Black Death? Around here?

EMMA. Are you in love with…?

HOMAIS. Me?

EMMA.…anyone?

HOMAIS. Not yet. But I'd keep your eyes peeled, if I were you.

The scene transforms to the top of a hill. Sunset. LÉON *sits, reading.* EMMA *approaches.*

Scene Twenty-three

EMMA. You're right. It's a perfect spot to watch the sun go down.

LÉON. Madame Bovary.

EMMA. Emma.

LÉON. It will be dark soon.

EMMA. Yes. I've noticed that tends to happen at the end of the day.

LÉON. How are you settling in?

EMMA. Charles has no patients.

LÉON. I understand camomile can help.

EMMA. Patients.

LÉON. Oh. I'll try to get ill.

EMMA. That would be appreciated. I very much enjoyed our conversation the other night.

LÉON. It made me feel alive. There's no one to talk to in Yonville. Not like that.

EMMA. There is now.

LÉON. Then it will make it worthwhile me staying.

EMMA. You were planning on leaving?

LÉON. I'm a boring clerk. I want to make something of my life.

EMMA. Me too.

LÉON. You? But you have done.

EMMA. Have I?

LÉON. You're married.

EMMA. Yes. My housekeeper tells me that marriage solves
everything.

LÉON. And...?

EMMA. It solves being unmarried.

LÉON. I have a book for you.

EMMA. For me? But you didn't know I'd be coming.

LÉON. I hoped you would be.

EMMA. I'm not sure what I have to give you in return.

LÉON. Nothing. The opportunity to talk to you.

EMMA. You have that, Léon. Whenever you like.

LÉON. Look at that sun.

EMMA. It's so orange.

LÉON. Really, really orange. And the sky is so blue.

EMMA. Double blue.

LÉON. It goes so well with the orange, don't you think?

EMMA. Yes. It's so intense.

LÉON. Dazzling.

EMMA. What does it mean?

LÉON. I don't know.

> LÉON *exits as* EMMA *peels off to approach* CHARLES,
> *who attaches a pregnancy bump to her. He cradles her.*
> LÉON *enters, sees them, and departs.*

Scene Twenty-four

Yonville Town Square.

EMMA. Léon. Léon!

> LÉON *turns.*

> I haven't seen you for ages. I've been to the hill. Have you been avoiding me?

LÉON. No.

EMMA. I have your book. It was beautiful. It made me cry.

LÉON. You never told me you were pregnant.

EMMA. Should I have done?

LÉON. Were you hiding it?

EMMA. Of course not. I didn't think to tell you.

LÉON. You didn't think to tell me? When we've divulged so much to each other over these months? I thought we were friends.

EMMA. Léon…

LÉON. I've clearly presumed too much.

EMMA. Léon, please. I didn't want you to know.

LÉON. Why not? Why?

EMMA. I don't know!

LHEUREUX. Madame Bovary? You are indeed as beautiful and as exquisite as I've been led to believe. My name is Monsieur Lheureux. My card.

EMMA. 'Monsieur Lheureux, merchant of luxury items and money-lender.'

LHEUREUX. A crude, but honest description.

LÉON. I have to go.

He leaves. EMMA *watches.*

LHEUREUX. I'd be more than happy to exhibit for you a few samples from my collection. I could come to your house now if that would suit?

Scene Twenty-five

LHEUREUX *begins to unpack items, beautiful silks, etc.*

LHEUREUX. The scarves are from Algeria, the embroidered linen from India.

EMMA. I love this.

LHEUREUX. Madame clearly has impeccable taste.

EMMA. How much?

LHEUREUX. A mere nothing. Twenty-six francs.

EMMA. Ah.

LHEUREUX. But there's no hurry; whenever is convenient.

JAVIER. So how did you feel about Léon?

EMMA. He shone like a beacon of hope.

JAVIER. You encouraged his affections.

EMMA. I was surprised to discover that he might love me.

JAVIER. Sounds a bit naive.

EMMA. What?

JAVIER. Well, it seems clear there was something subsexual going on.

EMMA. No. It was just thrilling.

She returns to LHEUREUX's *samples.* CHARLES *arrives, upbeat as usual.*

CHARLES. Emma?

EMMA. Charles, look at these beautiful things.

CHARLES. Emma, can I have a word?

They move aside.

We can't afford this to buy fanciful items like this.

EMMA. Oh, so I'm fanciful, am I?

CHARLES. That's not what I said.

EMMA *turns back.*

EMMA. Monsieur Lheureux, you'd better pack everything away. Apparently, we have no money.

CHARLES. That's not true.

EMMA. Then don't pack it away.

CHARLES. But things are a little tight.

EMMA. Pack it away.

CHARLES. I'm not saying pack it all away.

EMMA. Unpack.

CHARLES. Emma, I'm sorry.

EMMA. For what? What are you sorry for?

CHARLES. I don't know.

EMMA. Pack it all away.

CHARLES. Unpack the whole lot. We'll buy it all.

EMMA. Charles, it's too late now. I don't want it now!

CHARLES. Pack it all away. You heard her! And take the table with you.

They watch LHEUREUX *pack.* CHARLES *attempts to cover the awkwardness.*

I hear Léon is leaving Yonville.

EMMA. What?

CHARLES. Moving to Rouen.

EMMA. No!

CHARLES. I know – it's a shame, isn't it. Friendly chap.

EMMA. He can't!

CHARLES. Where are you going, Emma? You'll miss supper.

   EMMA *rushes out and runs into* HOMAIS *in the square.*

Scene Twenty-six

EMMA. Homais, where is he? Where's Léon?

HOMAIS. Left for the stagecoach. I'm going to miss him
   dreadfully.

EMMA. Léon!

   *She catches up with him. He steps up onto a small ladder (a
   coach).*

LÉON. Emma.

DRIVER (*voice-over*). Last coach to Rouen.

EMMA. What are you doing? You can't leave.

LÉON. Can't I? Why not?

EMMA. Because… I don't want you to.

LÉON. There's nothing for me here.

EMMA. There is.

LÉON. What would you say to keep me here?

EMMA. Must I say it aloud?

LÉON. Do you think I can read your mind?

EMMA. I don't know. Can you?

DRIVER (*voice-over*). Last call. Any more tickets?

LÉON. Emma, I've never told you how my heart races every time I see you. How my every thought contains you...

EMMA. Stop! How am I supposed to react to that? When you know the door is closed.

LÉON. That is not my doing.

EMMA. I know.

LÉON. Do you love Charles?

EMMA. What?

LÉON. Do you love him!?

EMMA. He's a kind man.

LÉON. That's not what I asked.

EMMA. He's my husband.

LÉON. Nor that.

EMMA. I don't know what love is!

> DRIVER *enters.*

DRIVER. We're about to set off, monsieur.

LÉON. You know perfectly well what love is, Emma!

> *They can't kiss.*

DRIVER. We can't wait any longer.

> LÉON *leaves.* EMMA *is left in a storm. Her distress turns to labour pains.* CHARLES *enters, realises the urgency and exits to fetch his bag. During a routine in which he tries to suitably prepare,* EMMA *gives birth, alone.*

CHARLES. It's a girl.

EMMA. Poor thing. What hope is there for a girl born into this world?

CHARLES *thinks she has made a joke. Then:*

CHARLES. I'm sorry? Oh, Emma, you must be exhausted. I know I am. Thank God I was here.

CHARLES *exits, cooing to baby Berthe. Bells chime and become the sound of a church interior. The* CURÉ *enters and watches* EMMA, *who prays.*

Scene Twenty-seven

Church. The sound of children playing, off.

CURÉ. Madame Bovary. You wanted to see me. How are you?

EMMA. Not well. I feel dreadful.

CURÉ. So do I. Must be the warmer weather. Surprising how it takes it out of you, isn't it. But then again, we are all born to suffer.

EMMA. Are we? Didn't Jesus do all that for us?

CURÉ. Some of it. Sorry, one moment. (*Shouting off.*) Clear off, you kids! (*To* EMMA.) Has your husband not been able to prescribe something for you?

EMMA. I don't think it's an earthly remedy I need. I want to ask you something.

CURÉ (*shouting off*). I said, clear off or I'll have you beaten! (*To* EMMA.) I won't really. And how is Monsieur Bovary? He and I must certainly be the two busiest men working in the parish – he tends the body, while I tend the soul.

EMMA. Right. I don't know if it's a confessional or just some spiritual guidance I need.

CURÉ. Although, having said that, only this morning I was asked to visit a cow that was blowing. Farmers do have a hard time of it, wouldn't you agree?

EMMA. They're not the only ones.

CURÉ. That's right. People in towns suffer dreadfully too.

EMMA. Sometimes I feel like I just want to end it all.

CURÉ. If only there was a switch, eh? It is tough for some people out there in our little community, isn't it.

ROBERT *enters*.

ROBERT (*laughing*). Curé, you'll never guess what. François has only held on to the bell rope again.

CURÉ. Again!?

ROBERT. You've got to come and look. His arse is wedged between the rafters.

CURÉ. Oh my goodness! I'll be right there. I'm just finishing up here. Was there anything else, Madame Bovary?

EMMA. Yes. I feel like I'm going out of my mind.

CURÉ. Absolutely. Me too. How can we cure the world? The thing is, we can't. Well, we can, but we've got to start at home. Have I approached you about the church-fête committee?

ROBERT. Curé, he's pulled himself up, but his trousers have come down!

The bell is clanging. Everyone is forced to raise their voices.

CURÉ. You know, I think God sends us things like this to cheer us up!

EMMA. Curé, can you hear me!? I desperately need help. I have severe melancholia.

CURÉ. Sophia who?

ROBERT. Curé! Quick!

CURÉ. Are you free on Tuesday evenings?

EMMA. I desperately need to talk to someone.

ROBERT (*off*). His belt's caught on the donger!

CURÉ. Madame Bovary, I have to see this!

He escapes. EMMA *breaks down.*

EMMA. Curé, my head feels like it's about to fucking explode!

CHARLES *enters with Berthe in a pram.*

CHARLES. Emma! I've been searching everywhere for you.

EMMA. Sorry. Choir practice.

CHARLES. Choir practice? Berthe wants you to say goodnight.

EMMA. Right.

CHARLES. Are you all right? Come here. You look exhausted.

EMMA. Oh, Charles. I'm so sorry.

CHARLES. What for, my love?

EMMA. You're so good to me. You deserve better than this. I'm going to make you happy.

CHARLES. But I am happy.

EMMA. Then I'll make us both happy.

They head upstage with the pram. CHARLES *takes it and exits.* JAVIER *appears, eating an apple.*

How could I have contemplated leaving her without a mother? That's what you want to ask, isn't it? There isn't an answer that would make any sense to you, that would make any sense to anyone.

JAVIER. Tell me about Rodolphe.

EMMA. Rodolphe Boulanger. Perhaps if I'd never met him.

The scene changes into CHARLES'*s surgery.* CHARLES *chalks 'Dr Bovary, MD' up on the wall.*

Scene Twenty-eight

GIRARD *is sat with his arm in a tourniquet.*

CHARLES. Emma, fetch some towels and a basin, will you, please?

EMMA *does so, along with the pram. When she returns,* RODOLPHE *is in the room.*

RODOLPHE. My man here has been complaining of uneasiness.

CHARLES. There's a man whose blood needs letting. This should settle him, Monsieur Boulanger.

CHARLES *makes the incision. Blood spurts from the back wall.* EMMA *collects it in a basin.*

RODOLPHE. That's remarkable work for a lady such as yourself. You don't get queasy?

EMMA. No. And I'm able to resist the urge to make sarcastic replies too.

RODOLPHE *steps out of the scene.* CHARLES *faints while performing the bloodletting.*

RODOLPHE (*to audience*). Very nice. Very nice, this doctor's wife. Pretty teeth, dark eyes, well turned out. Where can that clumsy oaf have found her? Poor little thing. She must be desperate for love, like a carp on a kitchen table gasping for water. Yet how to shake her off afterwards? I'll attend to that when the time comes. But firstly – how and where to meet? There will be that brat forever at her apron strings. And the maid, the neighbour, the husband. Ah, damn it, it'll take too long. But that pale complexion. I adore pale women. By Jove, of course – there's the agricultural fair! She's bound to attend – what else is there to do around here? It'll need a bold approach though or we'll be dilly-dallying around for months. And I want her! Now.

JAVIER. What a bastardo, no!

Scene Twenty-nine

The stage becomes the agricultural show. Actors play various animals, which becomes annoying for EMMA.

HOMAIS. Even though my expertise lies in pharmaceutical matters, I pride myself on being somewhat of an authority on agricultural matters too. I know, that's not for me to say – it's for other people to do that –

EMMA. But they don't.

HOMAIS. It follows, you see, that chemistry – being the study of reciprocal molecular action of all natural bodies – encompasses agriculture within its sphere. After all, what is the gradual fermentation of manure if it's not chemistry?

EMMA. Cow shit?

HOMAIS. Well, yes. But if you're interested in what's going on within the faeces...

EMMA. I'm not.

HOMAIS. That, I would say, is your loss.

EMMA. Blimey. Look at the size of that cock!

CHARLES *exits*. RODOLPHE *enters on the upper level*.

RODOLPHE. Madame Bovary.

EMMA. Monsieur Boulanger.

RODOLPHE. Or Rodolphe. Your choice.

EMMA. So, the fair tempted you off your fancy estate?

RODOLPHE. You've discovered where I live then?

EMMA. I got wind of it.

RODOLPHE. You'll have to come and visit.

EMMA. Will I?

RODOLPHE. You appear to be lacking an escort.

EMMA. My husband has just been distracted by a giant cock.

RODOLPHE *appears at stage level.*

RODOLPHE. How careless of him to leave you unattended.

EMMA. Oh, I'm very content to explore on my own.

RODOLPHE. Although you're unlikely to know the optimum vantage points.

EMMA. For what?

RODOLPHE. For the... unfolding events. Not least the fireworks that are about to... erupt. Come. I'll show you.

EMMA. I think I'll wait for Charles.

RODOLPHE. I shall be offended if you won't at least allow me to offer you the benefit of my insight.

EMMA. Which will benefit me... how?

RODOLPHE (*to audience*). I like her more and more. (*To* EMMA.) Then let me put it another way – what have you got to lose?

EMMA *departs on* RODOLPHE*'s arm.* CHARLES *appears.*

CHARLES. Emma! Emma? They've got giant peas too. Emma?

...then exits. EMMA *and* RODOLPHE *appear on the upper level. He lights a cigarette and hands it to her. He puts his hat on her head.*

EMMA. Look at all the town's firemen – all lined up with their buckets in case a spark should cause a little fire. And some excitement.

RODOLPHE. You're too good for Yonville, you know.

EMMA. Is that so?

RODOLPHE. I'm making you nervous.

EMMA. You underestimate me.

RODOLPHE. Is that so?

The fireworks begin. CHARLES *approaches, licking an ice cream.*

CHARLES. Emma. I was getting worried. Oh, you're wearing his hat.

He gives RODOLPHE *his hat back.*

RODOLPHE. Forgive me. I'm responsible for her absence, Dr Bovary.

CHARLES. No. Thank you for... for...

RODOLPHE. It was my pleasure. Emma was just saying how much she enjoys horse-riding.

EMMA. Was I?

CHARLES. Were you?

RODOLPHE. And I have some lovely geldings that are gagging to be exercised. I would be happy, with your permission of course, to take your wife out for a gallop.

CHARLES. Well, the air would no doubt do her good. What do you say, my love?

EMMA. I'm not so sure. I haven't ridden in a while.

RODOLPHE (*to audience*). She wants to come, she's just amazed her husband isn't protesting. (*To* EMMA.) Trust me – it's a wonderful way to see the woods.

EMMA. The woods?

CHARLES. I think you'll be in reliable hands with Monsieur Bollinger, darling.

RODOLPHE. Indeed she will. (*To audience.*) In very experienced hands.

Scene Thirty

JOHN *and* JONATHAN *create a woodland idyll with sounds and butterfly mobiles.* EMMA *and* RODOLPHE *enter the wood on 'horses'.*

RODOLPHE. I haven't been able to stop thinking about you since the fair. Perhaps your husband has a remedy.

EMMA. Don't make fun of me. Or him.

RODOLPHE. I'd rather cut out my tongue.

EMMA. Perhaps you should.

RODOLPHE. That's harsh. What are we to do about my condition?

EMMA. Nothing. We're riding.

RODOLPHE. Do you know that there are souls, constantly tormented, whose only cure is to throw themselves in to all manner of follies?

EMMA. I can imagine a society where such freedom is granted as equally to women as men.

RODOLPHE. But keeping to the subject, can you imagine the torment if nothing happens between you and I?

EMMA. Yes.

RODOLPHE. It will only be a matter of time, Emma.

EMMA. You flatter yourself.

RODOLPHE. Let's dismount.

EMMA. Here? Why?

RODOLPHE. I want to show you something.

They walk to a stream.

EMMA. It's a beautiful spot.

RODOLPHE. Listen. Can you hear the blackbird?

EMMA. Yes.

RODOLPHE. This is where the foxes come.

EMMA. Really?

RODOLPHE. I once watched a young male fox creep up upon a rabbit. He got closer and closer and the rabbit didn't move. It seemed as if she knew what was coming – as if she wanted to feel the fox near her, to feel the danger. And when he reached her, he gently picked her up in his jaw and trotted away with her into the woods.

She has walked towards him. He produces a trick bunch of flowers from under her crinoline.

EMMA. What are you doing?

RODOLPHE. When did you last feel passion? Real passion.

EMMA. Rodolphe. Please.

RODOLPHE. You thrill me, Emma. You excite me, you awaken me. I've never met anyone like you.

RODOLPHE *continues to perform tricks until* EMMA *is seduced. The sounds of nature grow.*

Emma. Are you really going to deny yourself this? This chance to feel alive. To feel delight. Pleasure. Danger.

Firecrackers, illuminated-thumb trick, handkerchief into a cane, appearance of trick foam balls...

I want you as much as you want me.

EMMA. I don't want you. (*Beat.*) I don't want to want you.

RODOLPHE. Why resist? Where will it lead? Your beauty engulfs me. Say you don't want this.

A kitten lands in his hand.

EMMA. I don't want this.

She gives in to the seduction. Nature sounds in full flow, like a hysterical jungle with additional trains going into tunnels, sirens, overture music, etc.

I have a lover! I have a lover!

End of Act One.

65

ACT TWO

Scene Thirty-one

JAVIER. Hola. Just while we're waiting for the last few to
come back in, I thought I might respond to a few topics that
came up in interval conversations – you wouldn't have
known it but I was mingling with you, disguised as an
Englishman. (*Produces notebook.*) And I listened in on quite
a few people saying that they wouldn't mind seeing the
scene in the woods again. The one with all the magic…

JOHN. Javier? What are you doing?

JAVIER. Responding to audience feedback.

JOHN. Have you been disguising yourself in the bar again?

JAVIER. Well, if you'd care to take an interest, I've picked up
some pretty useful feedback.

He hands the notebook to JOHN.

JOHN. 'Next time we should pre-order interval drinks.' Really
useful.

JAVIER. Skip down.

JOHN. 'I didn't know the Spaniard was also a magician.'

'I'd snog the Spaniard if he pulled flowers from under my
skirt.'

'I wouldn't mind seeing that Spaniard doing his tricks
again.'

'Me too.'

JAVIER. The public have voted.

JOHN. What? We're not doing the scene again.

EMMA. What's going on now?

JAVIER. Audience feedback. There's been an overwhelming response to the sex scene in the woods.

EMMA. I don't believe it.

JAVIER. You see – I tried to tell you all how sexy magic can be.

EMMA. No, I mean, why the hell are you making this all about sex?

JAVIER. I'm not. They are!

JONATHAN. That's pretty sexist actually, Javier.

EMMA. What? How is that sexist?

JONATHAN. Well…cos women aren't as interested in sex as men, so…

JOHN. Oh dear…

EMMA. Yes they are. They're just not as interested in crap sex.

JONATHAN. Which makes them less interested in sex overall. Just doing the math.

JOHN. What!? Why are we even discussing this? Can we please just get on with the second half?

JONATHAN. Good idea.

EMMA. Hang on. I've lost my focus now. I can't just – (*Clicks fingers.*) I'm not a performing seal.

JONATHAN. And she's not a seal either. Neither am I.

JAVIER. So. It seems like we're obliged to do the last scene again.

JOHN. No. We haven't got time.

JAVIER. In that case we'll just pick it up from the end. Emma, is that okay with you? Good. Go sound and lights.

The scene begins, as before, but the pace builds to a much quicker crescendo as JAVIER *attempts to perform all his tricks in time.*

RODOLPHE. Emma. Are you really going to deny yourself this? This chance to feel alive. To feel delight. Pleasure. Danger. I want you as much as you want me.

EMMA. I don't want you. (*Beat.*) I don't want to want you.

RODOLPHE. Why resist? Where will it lead? Your beauty engulfs me. Say you don't want this.

Another animal lands in his hand.

EMMA. I don't want this.

She gives in to the seduction. Nature sounds in full flow, like a hysterical jungle with additional trains going into tunnels, sirens, overture music, etc.

I have a lover! I have a lover!

Scene Thirty-two

We're suddenly inside – at home. EMMA turns on the chalked-up radio and dances to 'Chanson D'Amour'. CHARLES enters.

EMMA. Charles.

She switches off the radio.

CHARLES. Looks like someone had a good ride.

EMMA. Yes.

CHARLES. Did you go far?

EMMA. Further than expected.

CHARLES. It seems to have done you the world of good. You should go again.

EMMA. Really? What will people say?

CHARLES. Let their silly tongues wag if they must.

EMMA. Charles. I'd like to have control over my dowry.

CHARLES. Your dowry?

EMMA. Yes. It's so difficult to make sensible decisions with regards accounting and investments for our lives if I don't have a sense of our finances.

CHARLES. Now, Emma...

EMMA. Are you saying that I can't be trusted?

CHARLES. No. Of course not.

EMMA. Good. Then that's settled. Thank you, Charles.

CHARLES. I have to get going. Homais has a proposition he wants to discuss with me.

He exits.

JAVIER. So, you met Rodolphe again?

EMMA. Within twenty-four hours. He had awakened every cell inside me. I thought of nothing else apart from engineering circumstances to meet him. When Charles went off to work at first light, I would run to his house. Sometimes, as soon as Charles fell asleep, I would escape into the garden in my nightdress to meet him. Any time of day or night I would find a way to be with him. I fell in love. But I was to pay a price.

Scene Thirty-three

EMMA *is astride* RODOLPHE. *During the scene they move through a* Kama Sutra *choreography.*

EMMA. Why didn't you answer my last letter? Why did you leave me waiting?

RODOLPHE. Can you give me a chance to just...?

EMMA. No. Answer me!

RODOLPHE. Emma. I've been engaged in business.

EMMA. Oh. So this is to be my place, is it? To play second string to your business affairs? I will not be made to run after you, Rodolphe.

RODOLPHE. Look, try to be reasonable.

EMMA. Reasonable? Okay, fine. Since you choose to exercise indifference to me, I will choose to exercise indifference to you.

RODOLPHE. I was a few minutes late!

EMMA. Five hours! Do you think this is easy for me!? You told me not so long ago that you could never quench the thirst you had for me.

RODOLPHE. We've been lovers for months. We can relax a little, surely?

EMMA. Relax? Is that what you want? Because *that* is of no use to me.

RODOLPHE. No use to you? Who was the one who dragged you out of the darkness and into the light?

EMMA. How dare you!

RODOLPHE. Emma, I can bear no more of myself than I'm giving. Don't suffocate us. I don't need the constant flow of gifts from you. Nor do I need the doubt you express of my commitment. You have me.

EMMA. Really? Do I? Well, maybe I don't need you!

She leaves him in an awkward physical position.

RODOLPHE. Emma. Emma!

Scene Thirty-four

CHARLES *enters.*

CHARLES. Emma. I want your opinion.

EMMA. On what?

CHARLES. Homais has been reading a paper on the treatment and!? – as if! – cure of equinovarus talipes, or talipes equinovarus, I don't know.

EMMA. What?

CHARLES. Club foot.

EMMA. Oh.

HOMAIS *approaches* EMMA *privately.*

HOMAIS. Emma. I want your husband to perform an operation on Hippolyte. If successful, it will enhance Charles's reputation. And his income. He will be famous. But you'll need to convince him.

HOMAIS *exits.*

EMMA. Charles. Everyone will profit from this. Everyone will carry the tale of the great doctor from Yonville who first performed and executed this revolutionary procedure. I want to admire you.

CHARLES. You don't already?

EMMA. Of course I do. But this will secure us. It will secure you. It will help us to embrace our dreams. Charles, this is a challenge you should not retreat from. Our lives will change!

HIPPOLYTE *enters with a billiard cue.* CHARLES *turns the table to operating-table position.*

Hippolyte, you're a very brave man.

HIPPOLYTE. Brave? Do I need to be brave?

EMMA. You mustn't be afraid. It's a very simple procedure. After the Achilles tendon has been severed, and perhaps a few more…

HIPPOLYTE. A few more?

EMMA. Or those could be attended to later if things don't go according to plan.

HIPPOLYTE. Why wouldn't things go according to plan!?

EMMA. Well, you're not making things easy. Or rather, the specifics of your condition aren't. You're complicated. And you want to be cured, don't you? Of course you do. So. After the operation, your foot will be locked into the brace that Charles has had constructed…

HIPPOLYTE. What kind of brace?

CHARLES *produces a very scary looking leg-brace.*

EMMA. Stop worrying. Charles copied the design out of a magazine and made a few of his own modifications.

HIPPOLYTE. What!?

EMMA. Shh. The nuts and bolts are tightened or loosened every day, as he thinks best. Would you like me to sing to you?

She forces HIPPOLYTE *to sing 'Frère Jacques' and forces him to stay down where necessary. Meanwhile,* CHARLES *is searching through his bag.*

What is it, Charles?

CHARLES. I seem to have forgotten my scalpel.

EMMA. Charles!

CHARLES. I'll have to go back home.

HIPPOLYTE. I don't want to do it any more.

EMMA. Hippolyte, do you want to be a cripple for the rest of your life, or not? Haven't you got another knife?

CHARLES. No.

EMMA rummages in HIPPOLYTE*'s pockets.*

EMMA. How about this?

HIPPOLYTE. That's my penknife.

EMMA. Is it sharp?

HIPPOLYTE. Kind of.

CHARLES. Pass me that brandy.

She passes it to CHARLES. *He drinks from the brandy, cleans the penknife, crosses himself then makes the incision.* HIPPOLYTE *screams. There is a snap and then immediate relief. Everyone is stunned into silence.*

EMMA. Is that it?

CHARLES. I think so.

HIPPOLYTE. The relief! The pain has… gone.

EMMA. Charles!

CHARLES. We need to get the brace on immediately. Come along, Hippolyte.

CHARLES *exits with* HIPPOLTYE, *then re-enters looking stunned at what has happened.* EMMA *sees him in a new light, pushes him onto the table and straddles him.*

HOMAIS. You see. I told you it would work.

EMMA. You were right, Homais. Thank you.

HOMAIS. I have taken the liberty of penning an article to the media. With your endorsement, it will read thus…

EMMA *drags* CHARLES *home. She straddles him again, passionate with him at last.*

'On Tuesday, our little town of Yonville found itself the
scene of a revolutionary surgical operation, the success of
which will surely reach the history books. Monsieur Bovary,
one of our most distinguished practitioners – '

CHARLES. Oh, that is too much! Too much!

EMMA. No! Carry on. Carry on!

HOMAIS *exits*.

HOMAIS (*voice-over*). ' – he performed the operation as if
guided by magic. The patient complained of no pain.
Everything suggests that his convalescence will be brief.'

EMMA. Charles. I should like to have a whole new wardrobe.
It will reflect badly upon a doctor of your prowess to be
accompanied by a wife turned out in last year's fashions.
And what would *you* like?

CHARLES. Do you know what I'd really like?

LHEUREUX *enters the* BOVARYS' *house with an armful of
materials*.

EMMA. Lheureux!

CHARLES. I'd like to be valued.

LHEUREUX. Madame Bovary, I've brought you some sample
books from Paris... if you'd care to take a look...

EMMA. Yes.

LHEUREUX. Every society woman is clamouring for them.

EMMA. Yes!

LHEUREUX. I'd also be happy to offer you additional credit in
the light of your good fortune.

EMMA. Yes!!

LHEUREUX. I'll leave these samples for your perusal.

EMMA. Yes!!!

LHEUREUX *exits.* EMMA*'s ecstasy is punctured by another scream.*

VOICE (*off*). Help! He's dying! Send for a doctor!

HOMAIS *bursts in on* CHARLES *and* EMMA.

HOMAIS. Charles!

CHARLES. Homais, what is it!?

HOMAIS. Gangrene has set in on Hippolyte's leg. There are maggots in the wounds. The stench is putting people off their billiards.

VOICE (*off*). We need a doctor! A doctor who knows what he's doing!

EMMA *parts from* CHARLES. CAVINET *appears in a spotlight.*

CAVINET. Yonville is a two-hour ride from Rouen. I'll be there in an hour.

He enters the scene.

HOMAIS. Good afternoon.

CAVINET. Exactly. My name is Dr Cavinet. I solve problems.

HOMAIS. Good, because we've got one. My name is…

CAVINET *goes behind a wall then emerges.*

CAVINET. Okay, I've seen all I need to. Let's get down to brass tacks. The person who decided it was a good idea to operate on a man who was perfectly fit is an idiot. Straighten a club foot!? You might as well try levelling up a hunchback! This leg must be amputated.

HOMAIS. Right. I would stay for moral support. It's just that when you're an onlooker, the image works on the imagination as well as in reality, so it's kind of the most difficult position to be in.

CAVINET *smokes a cigarette as he begins sawing.*

CAVINET. You pharmacists are all the same, aren't you? Cooped up in your little shops, pontificating drivel. Look at me, in comparison: up at four every morning, I shave in cold water, sleep standing up and drink my own weewee.

That's why I'm better than you.

CAVINET *throws the removed leg to* CHARLES.

EMMA. What have I done? What have I done!

CAVINET. His stump will need dressing four times a day. Think you can manage that without risk of killing him again?

CHARLES. Yes.

CAVINET *exits*.

EMMA. To think that I have tried to love someone so... mediocre.

CHARLES. Emma. Everyone makes mistakes. Kiss me.

EMMA. Kiss you? Get away from me!!

She runs, desperate.

Rodolphe!

JAVIER. Why did you go back to him?

EMMA. Because I had to escape. From Charles. From his mother. From this whole town. From myself.

JAVIER. But Rodolphe is...

EMMA. I was blind. How was I to know he was about to betray me, about to make me feel as alone as it's possible to feel. He played with me – like a cat plays with a bird it has brought to the ground. And I believed every word he told me.

Scene Thirty-five

EMMA *throws herself into the arms of* RODOLPHE.

EMMA. Forgive me for turning away from you, Rodolphe. Run away with me.

RODOLPHE. Run away? But you have a daughter.

EMMA. We'll take her with us. Rodolphe, there are women more beautiful than me, but none that can love as I can. Do you believe me?

RODOLPHE. Yes, I can believe that.

EMMA. I will be everything to you. Family, country, everything. Do you love me? Swear it.

RODOLPHE. Do I love you?

EMMA. Swear it!

RODOLPHE. Emma, I adore you.

LHEUREUX *enters.* EMMA *turns to him.*

EMMA. Monsieur Lheureux, I need some items for travelling: I want a cloak, with a deep collar and a lining. And a silver-embossed purse.

LHEUREUX. Of course.

EMMA. And a trunk of Egyptian leather. And an initialled carpet bag. And some velvet gloves. Here is a list of the other items. I hope I can rely, as usual, on your discretion.

LHEUREUX. Your husband need know nothing of our dealings.

EMMA *turns back to* RODOLPHE.

EMMA. You've got the passports?

RODOLPHE. Yes.

EMMA. You haven't forgotten anything?

RODOLPHE. No.

EMMA. Are you sure?

RODOLPHE. Quite sure.

EMMA. And you'll be waiting for me at the Hotel de Provence at twelve o'clock tomorrow?

RODOLPHE. Twelve o'clock.

RODOLPHE *nods*.

EMMA. Until tomorrow then.

She runs off then turns back.

RODOLPHE. You have my word.

Scene Thirty-six

RODOLPHE *strides, contemplating*.

RODOLPHE. What an idiot I am. I can't leave the country. And saddle myself with a child?

Girard, take a letter!

GIRARD *enters*.

This is for her own good.

'Be brave, Emma. I don't want to ruin your life. Do you realise what an abyss I would have been dragging you to?'

Suppose I say I've lost all my money. No, she'd never believe that. How can one make such a woman listen to reason?

'I shall be forever devoted to you. But I fear that, one day, these ardent feelings of ours would cool. The agony I might suffer from your rejection. And the very thought of your suffering on account of my suffering is torture to me.

'And how might society have reacted to us? They might have snubbed you – insulted you. You that I would set upon a

throne. Therefore I have decided to leave the country to prevent all the harm I may do to you.

'*Keep a place in your heart for this unhappy man who has lost you. Adieu. Your... friend, Rodolphe.*'

GIRARD *has started crying*

Ah, Girard. Useful. Nice idea. Place the letter at the bottom of a basket of apricots and make sure they are delivered personally to Madame Bovary early tomorrow.

The basket is taken to EMMA. *She finds the letter and goes to the top of the house. She opens a window, about to jump.* CHARLES *enters below.*

CHARLES. Emma, where are you? It seems we won't be seeing Monsieur Rodolphe for a while. He's taking a trip abroad apparently.

I don't blame him to be honest. He has money, he's a bachelor.

Sound effects of a trap clattering past.

There he goes now, in fact. Off in his blue tilbury. These apricots are delicious – like they're filled with the sun. Would you like one? Emma?

He suddenly sees EMMA.

Emma!

He catches her before she throws herself out of the window.

Emma! Emma, speak to me. What is it? What's happened?

CHARLES*'s* MOTHER *enters.*

EMMA. Life is a dark corridor with a bolted door at the far end.

MOTHER. Okay, this is getting ridiculous now.

CHARLES. Mother, please! Not now.

MOTHER. Then when? She'll be the ruin of you, you mark my words. She clearly can't supervise this house. Were you aware that your maid, Félicité – who is supposed to be in your wife's charge – has been receiving a gentleman caller?

CHARLES. I didn't know that. I will take her in hand.

EMMA (*screaming*). Are you not even going to stand up to her, Charles? What possible society are we living in where even the housemaid isn't allowed a little bit of joy! Get out. Get out! Get out!!!

They leave. JAVIER enters.

JAVIER. So, did you see Rodolphe again?

EMMA, *calm, doesn't move.* JAVIER *starts to become concerned.*

Huh? So did you see Rodolphe again? Tell me about how great Charles was. Didn't you remember him playing with Berthe? Emma? Emma Fielding?

EMMA *exits.* JAVIER *is confounded. Left on his own, he puts on the cloak that* EMMA *has discarded and becomes her.*

CHARLES (*voice-over*). Emma? Emma?

CHARLES/JOHN *enters and discovers* JAVIER *dressed as 'Emma'.*

Emma?

JAVIER. Hello, Charles. I want to see you play with Berthe... in a happy way – (*Puts his hand over his mouth.*) Daddy!

Now they are simply trying to save the show.

Life is like a corridor with a dark door at the end.

CHARLES. I have something for you.

JAVIER. What is it? Opera tickets?

CHARLES. Yes. Actually –

JAVIER. Charles, how wonderful. Lucia Semolina.

CHARLES. Yes. *Lucia di Lammermoor* in Rouen.

JAVIER. Life is like... a room without a view.

CHARLES. How did I afford them, you wonder?

JAVIER. Do I?

CHARLES. Yes you do.

JAVIER. And I will need a new dress. Won't I?

EMMA *appears*.

Oh. A mirror.

CHARLES. Emma. You're back.

EMMA. Can we stop for a moment, please. I'm sorry, John.
Everyone. I need to explain what happened just then. I
should say that I've never walked offstage like that before.
And it wasn't about me. It was actually about Emma.

JOHN. Bovary?

EMMA. Yes. You see, for those of you that don't know – and
it's very important to me that you don't get the wrong
impression of Emma... Bovary – after Rodolphe leaves, she
spends six weeks in almost total reclusion. In fact, great
chunks of her life are spent alone, desperately alone,
desperate to find... solace. And I don't want to give people
the impression that she just leapt from Rodolphe to Léon like
some hysterical nymphomaniac. She's ill. I couldn't do that
to her and so I... well – you saw.

JAVIER. Emma, I'm not a dramaturg but I think dramatising six
weeks of silence is going to be a bit boring.

EMMA. Jonathan! What are you doing?

JONATHAN *is stood in a dinosaur costume*.

JONATHAN. I probably missed the moment now. Initially, it
was to create a distraction from... this. Found it backstage.
Bad decision?

EMMA. You did your best.

JOHN. Of course it's a bad decision! You're dressed as a
fucking dinosaur in the middle of a period French tragedy.

JAVIER. John, I think you need to calm down. You're in danger of completely derailing the show with that kind of outburst.

JOHN. Me!!!?

EMMA. John, it's all fine. We'll just pick up from where we got to.

JAVIER. What a privilege it is for any drama students out there in the audience, to be experiencing the strings of live theatre.

EMMA. Javier, take off the dress, Jonathan, get out of that dinosaur costume. Ladies and gentlemen, I want you to imagine, in your mind's eye, that Emma Bovary is emerging from a long period of deep depression, followed by inertia and boredom and an attempt again to connect with her daughter and make her marriage work. (*To lighting box.*) Thank you, Roxanne.

Lighting state is restored.

BERTHE (*voice-over*). Daddy?

EMMA (*back into character*). Charles, go to Berthe. I want to watch the two of you play.

CHARLES. Emma, I have something for you.

EMMA. Opera tickets! *Lucia di Lammermoor* in Rouen!? Box seats?!

CHARLES. I had some money put by.

EMMA. But these must be like gold dust.

CHARLES. Well... I pulled some strings.

EMMA. Really? What strings? How?

CHARLES. Well... actually they happened to have some returns.

EMMA. Oh, Charles. Do you think I'm up to it?

CHARLES. We'll make damn sure you're up to it.

EMMA. I shall need to find something to wear.

She exits.

LHEUREUX. Monsieur Bovary. I wonder if I might have a word?

CHARLES. What is it, Monsieur Lheureux?

LHEUREUX. It's just a small matter. I did promise to your wife I'd be discreet, but owing to her condition...

CHARLES. Yes?

LHEUREUX. She owes me some money. For some luggage and...

CHARLES. Luggage?

LHEUREUX. Women must be allowed their little secrecies.

CHARLES. She's not been well.

Scene Thirty-seven

Horse carriages clatter, a poster advertising the opera is wheeled in. EMMA *looks out of a hotel window in Rouen as she dresses, excited.*

EMMA. Look, Charles, it seems as if the whole of Rouen is dressed up.

CHARLES. The end. (*Snaps book shut.*) Wow, so both Lucia and her lover end up dead. Why do all operas have to end in tragedy?

EMMA. It's one of the most romantic pieces of work ever written.

CHARLES. All that misunderstanding though. And secrecy. More stressful than romantic, I'd say.

EMMA. Can you tie my lace, Charles?

CHARLES. Did I mention that I love you as much now as I did on our wedding day?

EMMA. Yes. You did.

CHARLES. Good. (*Offers his hand.*) Madame Bovary? Shall we?

The scene transforms to the opera. They're sitting in a box.
EMMA is transfixed. CHARLES's attention begins to
wander. He sees someone in the audience and grabs the
opera glasses from EMMA. The opera is loud. EMMA can't
hear him. He shouts exactly at the moment the volume drops.

It's Léon!

The music starts up again. EMMA is in shock. The act ends
to great applause.

Let's go to the bar. We'll probably run into him.

They move to the interval bar. CHARLES tries to get served.
LÉON appears upstage of EMMA. She turns. They look at
each other across a crowded room. CHARLES gives up.

This is useless. No one's taking the slightest bit of interest in
me. Léon! There he is.

LÉON. Monsieur Bovary.

CHARLES. How wonderful to see you. Did you not see him,
Emma – you were staring right at him.

EMMA. This is indeed unexpected.

CHARLES. I've been trying to get some drinks. It's madness
here.

LÉON. There's a café just on the quayside. I sometimes go
there.

Scene Thirty-eight

A café forms around them. Accordion. JOHN *slides in a table.*

LÉON. Ah. Waiter, could you bring us some drinks, please?

CHARLES. What? No, it's me. Charles.

LÉON. Of course. Sorry, it's the light.

CHARLES. But I will organise us some drinks.

CHARLES *exits.*

LÉON. How long are you in Rouen?

EMMA. Just for the night.

LÉON. Emma, I can't disappear from your life again.

EMMA. You were never gone from it.

LÉON. Destiny is offering us a second chance.

EMMA. Léon…

LÉON. I must see you.

EMMA. Léon, I haven't been well.

CHARLES *returns with some drinks.*

CHARLES. There we go.

LÉON. Thank you. And could you bring us the bill as well, please?

CHARLES. No, Léon. It's me. Charles.

LÉON. Of course it is! The way you're dressed though.

CHARLES. Sorry, yes. My fault. How did you enjoy the first two acts? I was rather drawn in.

LÉON. I have to confess that after hearing Rubini, Persiani and Grisi sing recently, I was a little underwhelmed with Legardy.

CHARLES. Yes. Me too. Which one is he?

LÉON. He's playing Edgardo.

CHARLES. Yes. Which one is he?

LÉON. The lover.

CHARLES. Ah yes. Voice like a foghorn. And she was somewhat over-egging the tragedy with all that hair swishing about, eh? It's nearly time. We should get our skates on.

LÉON. To be honest, I wouldn't rush back to see the last act. I saw it a few nights ago and the hair swishing becomes ridiculous. As does the opera. I suspect they've already begun now anyway.

CHARLES. We'll probably be all right if we knock these back, won't we?

EMMA. I'd rather not rush, Charles.

CHARLES. Right. No, of course not. It's just that they were quite expensive.

LÉON. All the more reason not to rush them.

CHARLES. I meant the tickets.

LÉON. If you were to extend your stay I could organise complimentary tickets for tomorrow night.

EMMA. Really?

LÉON. I can pull some strings.

CHARLES. Ah. I'm afraid we have to get back. Well, I do. But you could stay on, Emma?

LÉON. The last act is beautiful.

CHARLES. I thought you said it was ridiculous.

LÉON. No.

CHARLES. Oh. I must have misunderstood. Well, it's your choice, Emma.

LÉON. I could show you the sights of Rouen. I'm an excellent guide.

CHARLES. Now *there's* an offer. I think you should stay, my love. Don't worry about me.

LÉON. So, it's settled then. We could meet at the cathedral. Shall we say noon? Are you sure you can't come, Charles?

CHARLES. I'm afraid not.

LÉON. That is a shame.

The conversation continues over the hubbub of sudden café rowdiness. EMMA walks away. She writes a letter. Upstage, LÉON waits inside the cathedral. A clock reads 12.25. EMMA enters with the letter.

Scene Thirty-nine

Cathedral.

LÉON. I thought you weren't coming.

EMMA. I'm not staying.

LÉON. But you must.

EMMA. Léon, time has moved on. I came to give you this – (*Letter.*)

LÉON. Emma, please. If we don't receive love from the ones who are meant to love us then we will never stop looking for it.

EMMA. Don't make this hard.

LÉON. I often think I see you at street corners, sometimes I go chasing after a cab because I've caught sight of a shawl or a veil like yours…

EMMA. Stop! I'm too old for this and you are too young. I longed for you too, Léon. But that time has vanished.

LÉON. I don't believe that.

EMMA. I'm married.

LÉON. I love you.

EMMA. Just read this... no, don't.

BEADLE. Good morning. Welcome to the cathedral? Your first time?

EMMA. Yes.

LÉON. No.

BEADLE. Then let me offer you some insight. The simple stone behind you covers Pierre de Brézé, governor of Normandy, who died at the battle of Monterey on the 16th of July, 1465.

LÉON. Well, it's been a fascinating tour, but now we must...

BEADLE. And on your right, this gentleman on the horse, is his grandson, Louis de Brézé. Now, to the left...

LÉON. The Holy Virgin. Thank you.

BEADLE. Below your feet here is the tomb of Richard Cœur de Lion. Guess how much it weighs?

LÉON. I couldn't care less. Just take this and go.

The BEADLE *ignores the money he is being offered.*

BEADLE. Forty thousand kilos.

LÉON. Emma, this way...

BEADLE. Wait. You can't leave until you've seen the steeple, I insist.

LÉON. Great. Lead the way.

He goes through a door and starts to climb stairs.

BEADLE. It is four hundred and forty feet high, nine less than the great pyramid of Egypt.

LÉON *slams and locks the door on him while* JOHN *pushes on the carriage.*

EMMA. Léon, you can't.

LÉON. I can. Come on.

EMMA. Where are we going?

BEADLE. Hey! Let me out!

They run outside.

LÉON. Driver! Over here.

CAB DRIVER. Probably easier if you come over here. Where to, sir?

LÉON. Wherever you like. Get in, Emma.

EMMA. Léon...

LÉON. One afternoon. That's all I ask of you.

They're inside.

Drive!

CAB DRIVER. But where to?

LÉON. A tour of Rouen.

They set off.

Scene Forty

[*This scene can be played with two* CAB DRIVERS, *enjoying the double entendres between them*.]

CAB DRIVER. We're currently on Rue Grand-Pont. On your left you'll notice the Quai Napoléon, the Pont Neuf, and our first stop will be at the great erection of Pierre Corneille.

EMMA. Oh, Léon!

LÉON. Go on, driver! No stops.

CAB DRIVER. We're looking up at the Carrefour Lafayette and the famous trimmed bushes of the Jardin des Plantes.

LÉON. Slower!

EMMA. No, speed up!

CAB DRIVER. To your right, the great opening of La Grande-Chaussée, that we can pause at if you like.

EMMA. Go inside!

CAB DRIVER. I'm not sure we're allowed inside.

LÉON. Don't stop!

CAB DRIVER. We'll soon be approaching the fountains of Quai aux Meules, that pump water twenty feet into the air. You want to see that?

EMMA. Take me.

CAB DRIVER. In the distance, the famous domes of the Place du Champ de Mars. Domes. Do you want to see the domes?

LÉON. No. I'll pay you double! Triple!

CAB DRIVER. There's Château Humpington.

EMMA. Yes!

CAB DRIVER. Hornpipe Drive.

LÉON. Yes!

CAB DRIVER. Bone Lane.

EMMA. Yes!

CAB DRIVER. And a magnificent view of the sausage factory.

LÉON. More!

CAB DRIVER. I can't think of any more.

LÉON. Just keep going!

CAB DRIVER. The back entrance of the train station?

EMMA. Yes!

CAB DRIVER. The postal receiving office.

LÉON. Emma!

CAB DRIVER. I'm running out! A manhole cover?

EMMA. Yessss!

CAB DRIVER. A French Revolution cannon?

EMMA. Léon!! (*Screams.*)

LÉON. I love you!

CAB DRIVER. Blimey, you're certainly keen sightseers.

LÉON. Again! Go anywhere you can think of. Just keep going.

The music drowns out the CAB DRIVER's *speech.*
Exhausted, using his inhaler, he almost falls from his perch.

CAB DRIVER. That's it! That is enough! Six hours is enough
sightseeing!

EMMA exits. LÉON *tips the* CAB DRIVER *and pats him on
the back.*

LÉON. Fascinating. I never knew there were so many points of
interest.

Scene Forty-one

EMMA *walks*. CHARLES *enters*. *Home*.

CHARLES. Emma. How was Rouen?

EMMA. Not what I was expecting.

CHARLES. And the final act?

EMMA. Devastating.

CHARLES. I thought we might have an early bath? What do you say?

EMMA. I'm so tired, Charles.

CHARLES. Of course. I should have thought. I'll make you a bedtime drink.

   CHARLES *exits*. JAVIER *enters*.

EMMA. This is when the final and cruellest deception of Charles began. And at a time when he most needed me.

   CHARLES *enters*.

   Charles? What is it?

CHARLES. I've just received a telegram. My father's dead.

EMMA. Oh, Charles.

CHARLES. While we were in Rouen. I didn't get to see him.

   She takes him in her arms. He cries onto her lap.
   LHEUREUX *enters*.

LHEUREUX. Madame Bovary. Have you considered the position you are in?

EMMA. I'm sorry?

LHEUREUX. Word reaches me that recent and unfortunate events have resulted in your husband inheriting a small country property.

EMMA. It began by my taking power of attorney over his inheritance.

LHEUREUX. The sale of it could allow you not only to attend your debts to me but also look at... investing further in the standard of living you clearly enjoy.

EMMA. And so it was done. Charles was easily persuaded into agreement and then I became... free.

EMMA *begins to play the piano.* LÉON *writes at a desk. Split stage.*

LÉON. '*How did I love before I knew you, before I possessed your affection? You may reckon upon my love as something that is to endure when everything that can perish has perished. I love you without question, without calculation, without reason. My happiness is to be near you. Incessantly. Your kisses inject me with life. When can you next come to Rouen?*'

CHARLES. I haven't had such a treat in a long time. It sounds great.

EMMA. Oh. I couldn't be more rusty.

CHARLES. No, play it again.

She plays badly.

EMMA. You see?

CHARLES. Huh. Sounded better before.

EMMA. A fluke. I'd think about lessons but that'd be far too extravagant.

CHARLES. No, no. Madame Belen de Français just down the road is a brilliant teacher apparently.

EMMA. No, not her.

CHARLES. Monsieur Dimat, next door?

EMMA. No.

CHARLES. Well, in that case how about...

EMMA. I will need to go to Rouen to find a decent teacher.

CHARLES. Rouen?

EMMA. Yes. Regularly.

CHARLES. Right. Well, once a month shouldn't hurt.

EMMA. More like once a week.

CHARLES. Right. Well, you know what's best.

EMMA. No, you do, Charles. If you think I should make the journey to Rouen, once a week, or twice a week if necessary, then I'll do it.

CHARLES. I don't want to put a strain on you, Emma.

EMMA. It won't be a strain if I perhaps stay the night on occasion.

CHARLES. Of course. All that makes… total sense to me.

EMMA. Thank you, Charles.

Montage. EMMA *gets up and crosses to where* LÉON *is waiting for her. They embrace.* CHARLES *sits at the piano. The music continues.* EMMA *returns home with boxes of finery handed to her by* LHEUREUX. *She meets* LHEUREUX *again on her way back out to meet* LÉON. *She takes presents to him.*

LHEUREUX. I have the advance on the sale of your father-in-law's property. Minus the standard fees and commissions, it amounts to one thousand eight hundred francs.

EMMA. And how much do I already owe you?

LHEUREUX. Four thousand francs. I thought you might find things easier if I was to divide the debt into four individual sums, with a small amount of interest, which can't be avoided of course. Sign them. And then you'll be free to concentrate on your 'music lessons'.

EMMA *walks away in shock. She returns to* LÉON.

LÉON. How did he find out?

EMMA. I don't know. It doesn't matter.

LÉON. We could change location.

EMMA. No. I love this room. Our room.

LÉON. Why are you even doing business with that rat?

EMMA (*angry*). Because without him, none of this would be possible, Léon. Did you ever wonder how I paid for all this!?

LÉON. What is your situation, Emma?

EMMA. I don't want to talk about it. Kiss me.

EMMA *returns to* CHARLES *and sits at the piano.*

Scene Forty-two

Home.

CHARLES. How are the lessons going? You don't seem to practise much at home.

EMMA. I practise when I'm alone.

CHARLES. Right. Isn't it Mademoiselle Lempereur who teaches you?

EMMA. Yes. Why?

CHARLES. Nothing. Only I visited her mother on a call-out today and she happened to be there. Oddly she had no recollection of you. I'm sure there must be several Mademoiselle Lempereurs who teach the piano in Rouen. Scores of them in fact.

EMMA. Are you seriously expecting me to bear the burden of your suspicion and mistrust, Charles? I've got receipts if you must know. Look. I'll show you.

CHARLES. Emma, there's really no need.

EMMA. They'll be here somewhere. I'll find them!

CHARLES. Emma, please stop. I'm not asking to see receipts.

EMMA. I'll find them!

CHARLES. Look at this. This looks like one. There – the matter is settled. Let's go out. Shall we go out? You could wear your new dress.

EMMA. What new dress?

CHARLES. The yellow one. It arrived today.

EMMA. What were you doing receiving that!?

CHARLES. I just answered the door.

EMMA. Why were you even here?

CHARLES. Emma, I live here.

EMMA. Charles!

CHARLES. I haven't seen it. There isn't a dress.

EMMA. So why did you mention it?

CHARLES. I don't know.

EMMA. Is there a dress or not?

CHARLES. There is. But I don't know why it's here. It's a mystery.

EMMA. What?

CHARLES. I'm not having an affair.

EMMA. Charles, please stop. It was simply a surprise for you.

CHARLES. Then let me buy you another one.

EMMA. No.

CHARLES. I'd like to. In fact, I insist.

EMMA *walks towards* LÉON.

EMMA. Tell me you love me.

CHARLES. I love you.

Scene Forty-three

Hotel room.

LÉON. I swear that I will love and worship you until the end of my days.

EMMA. Ha. You're a man. That will be beyond you. You'll marry.

LÉON. I won't.

EMMA. You're all villains. *I* must keep this alive. Somehow.

LÉON. Emma, the money…

EMMA. I don't want to talk about it!

  LHEUREUX *enters.*

LHEUREUX. But you must. Did you think, my little lady, that I was going to carry on supplying you with goods and credit until the end of time? Out of the sheer goodness of my heart? The court will uphold my rights.

EMMA. I'll pay you the money. I just need time.

LHEUREUX. You've had time.

EMMA. This isn't fair!

LHEUREUX. Isn't it? Is it fair that the likes of me slave here while the likes of you go off enjoying yourself? The world has hungers of its own, Madame Bovary.

EMMA. Don't preach to me.

LHEUREUX. It never did any harm.

EMMA. I'll sign something.

LHEUREUX. I've had enough of your signatures.

EMMA. I'll sell something!

LHEUREUX. You've nothing left to sell. Apart from, that is, your house.

EMMA. Monsieur Lheureux, there must be some other way!

LHEUREUX. Well. Perhaps we *could* find a way for you to...
recompense.

He puts his hand up to touch her. She swipes it away.

EMMA. Get away from me! I am not to be bought!

LHEUREUX. I pity you.

EMMA *turns. A carriage clatters past. She watches it depart.*

EMMA. Rodolphe? Rodolphe!

*She runs. Montage. She has a silent discourse (music covers)
with CHARLES and then LÉON, and is then handed a letter.*

Scene Forty-four

EMMA. What's this?

LHEUREUX. You no longer owe me any money.

EMMA. You've cleared my debt?

LHEUREUX. Indeed I have. It's now someone else's problem.

EMMA. No! You promised me you wouldn't sell it on!

LHEUREUX. But I was forced. I had the knife at my throat.

EMMA. Six thousand francs?!

LHEUREUX. And a warrant to assess the contents of your
house, I would imagine.

She returns to LÉON. She pours champagne into his mouth.

LÉON. That's enough. I have to work in the morning.

EMMA. Do you love me?

LÉON. You know I do.

EMMA. Say it!

LÉON. I love you.

EMMA. Would you do anything for me?

LÉON. You know I would.

EMMA. I need six thousand francs.

LÉON. What!?

EMMA. You can get it.

LÉON. How?

EMMA. You work for a firm of lawyers. They must have safes full of money.

LÉON. You're asking me to steal from my employers?

EMMA. I'm asking you to help me. I've sacrificed everything for you!

LÉON. But... Emma, you're asking too much of me. If I was to do this...

EMMA. Too much of you?

She pulls out a letter and starts to read.

'*You may reckon upon my love as something that is to endure when everything that can perish, has perished!*'

LÉON. You're crazy.

EMMA. At last! A diagnosis. Thank you!

She turns and leaves and runs.

Scene Forty-five

EMMA *arrives at her house. The* BAILIFFS *are knocking at the door. She considers and then begins to run again. She arrives at* RODOLPHE's. *She finds him sitting in a chair. Asleep. She composes herself.*

EMMA. Rodolphe?

He wakes.

RODOLPHE. It's you.

EMMA. You've returned.

RODOLPHE. I was going to get in touch.

EMMA. Has life been kind to you in the last three years?

RODOLPHE. Neither kind nor unkind.

EMMA. It might have been better if we'd stayed together.

RODOLPHE. I've often wondered the same.

EMMA. If only you had known how much you meant to me.

RODOLPHE. Can you forgive the coward I was?

EMMA. Quite possibly. It seems to be an unavoidable condition of the stronger sex. Is there another woman?

RODOLPHE. No.

EMMA. My feelings haven't changed.

RODOLPHE. I've been so foolish. I don't think I can ever stop loving you, Emma.

He kisses her. She retracts.

What is it?

EMMA. Nothing.

RODOLPHE. Tell me.

EMMA. I need money. I'm ruined.

RODOLPHE. Is that why you came here?

EMMA. No. Partly. A few hundred francs will keep the bailiffs away.

RODOLPHE. Emma, I don't have it.

EMMA. What?

RODOLPHE. I haven't got it.

EMMA. You haven't got it?

She looks around.

When people are poor they don't put silver on the butts of their guns or have trinkets for their watches!

She rips his pocket watch from him and hurls it at the wall.

I might have spared myself this final humiliation. I would have given you everything, Rodolphe; worked with my hands, begged in the streets – just for a smile, just for a glance, just to hear you say thank you. Right here in this room you once knelt at my feet and vowed me an eternity of love. And I believed you. I believed your lies! You ripped my heart in two, Rodolphe. You might at least have had the decency to send me away after you'd fucked me that first time. My life might have been happier then. And now I come begging to you for help. And you turn me away.

RODOLPHE. Emma. I don't have it.

She turns. She's alone. Night. Wind.

EMMA. The earth beneath my feet, more yielding than the sea. The furrows, like immense brown waves breaking into foam. The cow-plank, the footpath, the alley, the market, the chemist's shop.

She stumbles. She bangs on the pharmacy door.

Justin. Open up. Quickly.

JAVIER. Emma, that's passed. It's gone.

EMMA. Justin. It's an emergency!

JAVIER. You're with me – in The Golden Lion. Remember?

As if off-script.

EMMA. No I'm not.

JAVIER. Yes… you are. Your husband is crossing the Square.

CHARLES *enters.*

CHARLES. Emma, I know everything. It's all going to be okay. We have this man and his friend to thank. They have offered to pay off enough of the debt to keep the bailiffs away. And as for my reputation…

EMMA. John.

CHARLES. We'll move. I'll set up somewhere else.

EMMA. John. I'm really sorry to stop again but… this isn't right. Think about it; two rat-catchers change the destiny of Madame Bovary by paying off some debts?

JOHN. And buying up all the arsenic.

JAVIER. Even I have to admit, that's not bad for a plot device. For John, anyway.

EMMA. No, you're missing the point. It doesn't matter how good or bad the idea is. Even if John came up with the most brilliant idea in the world…

JAVIER. That's not going to happen.

EMMA. We can't *save* Emma Bovary with a plot device. Her destiny has been decided – alongside the many other fictional nineteenth-century female protagonists driven to suicide by male writers, I might add. What's next? You save Anna Karenina from throwing herself under a train by… I don't know…

JAVIER. A particularly vigilant engineer?

EMMA. Exactly.

JAVIER. At the last minute he yanks down the lever on the signal box and diverts the train. They end up falling in love and moving to Moscow…

EMMA. No, I didn't mean…

JAVIER. Leaves on the line? You'd actually be spoilt for choice with that title.

JOHN. Javier!

JAVIER. I'm just saying, it would send audiences away with a bit of a spring in their step.

EMMA. But if you deny Madame Bovary her death, you kill her.

JAVIER. Wow. That's… pretty profound. John, I hope you're taking this in.

JONATHAN. At last someone's finally articulated what I've been thinking all along.

JAVIER. What are you talking about!?

JONATHAN. Feminism. I'm not embarrassed to admit to being one.

JOHN. So. What now?

EMMA. We do the ending that we should have rehearsed.

JAVIER. As accustomed as I am to a bit of improvisation, I have to admit – that's a brave decision.

JOHN. You mean, without the back wall flying out to reveal Paris?

EMMA. Yes.

JAVIER. So we're cutting me coming in on a bicycle with the onions and the baguette?

EMMA. Yes.

JAVIER. Shame.

JONATHAN. The cancan dance?

JOHN. Yes, Jonathan, I think we're probably cutting the cancan.

JAVIER. What about my Marcel Marceau impression?

EMMA. No!

JOHN. We're cutting the whole montage. She's right. Jonathan, put on Justin's apron and get the arsenic from the props table. Roxanne, if you can try and busk this, that's be great.

JAVIER. So, what do I do?

JOHN. 'She stood in a daze…' We can go from that speech.

JAVIER. She stood in a daze.

JOHN. No, hang on. Wait for the lights.

Lighting and sound effects as appropriate.

JAVIER. Now?

JOHN. Yes.

JAVIER. She stood in a daze. Memories, came rushing forth like a thousand explosions. Her father, her mother, the room she grew up in. In an sudden ecstasy of fearlessness, that made her almost joyous, she ran down the hill, crossed the cow-plank, the footpath, the alley, the market square, and reached the pharmacy.

EMMA *bangs on the door.*

EMMA. Justin. Open up. Quickly. Justin!

The door opens.

JUSTIN. Madame Bovary!? I'm afraid the pharmacy is closed.

EMMA. It's an emergency.

JUSTIN. The doctor was looking for you earlier. Did he find you? There were bailiffs…

EMMA *(fainting)*. Oh God…

JUSTIN. Here? Sit down. I'll get you some water.

EMMA. No. I'm fine. I just need your keys to the cabinet.

JUSTIN. The cabinet? Why?

EMMA. Shhh. Don't worry. It's all going to be fine. Where are they? Where do you keep them? Tell me, Justin?

JUSTIN. They're in my pocket.

EMMA. This pocket?

JUSTIN. Yes.

EMMA. Thank you.

JUSTIN. If you tell me what it is you need…

She crosses to the cabinet and takes out a jar of arsenic.

Madam Bovary, no!

EMMA. Don't come near me, Justin!

She plunges her hand into the jar and eats a handful of arsenic.

JUSTIN. Why!?

EMMA. If I could explain it in words then I would. But human speech is like a cracked kettle on which we tap crude rhythms while we long to make music that will melt the stars.

The BLIND MAN *begins to play.* EMMA *walks past and stops. She finds a coin, throws it into his hat. She then collapses, clutching her chest, retching in pain. She manages to get back to her feet, stumbling.*

Scene Forty-six

CHARLES. Emma!

He catches her. Lights close in on them.

EMMA. The bailiffs took everything then?

CHARLES. Apart from my medical bag.

EMMA. How merciful.

CHARLES. I know everything, Emma.

EMMA. You don't know everything, my love. Tomorrow you'll find my letter.

CHARLES. I should have done more. I could have done more.

EMMA. No, Charles, you did everything you could have done. You couldn't have made me happier.

CHARLES. I could have taken you to Paris.

EMMA. No.

CHARLES. The Arc de Triomphe.

EMMA. Stop.

CHARLES. Notre-Dame Cathedral.

EMMA. Charles, no. There's nothing that you, or anyone else could have done. I know that now.

CHARLES. Hold my hand.

EMMA *takes his hand.*

Close your eyes. We're walking into the Louvre. Can you see that? Can you see that we're walking into the Louvre?

Pause.

And now we're walking along the banks of the Seine. Can you see the water, Emma?

EMMA. Yes.

CHARLES. And the boats?

EMMA. Yes.

CHARLES. And what else? What can you see?

EMMA. I can see... La Sainte-Chapelle in the distance. The Montmartre. And the cobbled streets of the Marais.

CHARLES. And cafés.

EMMA. Yes. We can sit in cafés. And visit dress shops.

CHARLES. As many dress shops as you like. And stroll down the Champs-Élysées.

EMMA. The Champs-Élysées. Like a golden fruit suspended beneath some fantastic bough.

Pause.

CHARLES. I would like to have shown you all that.

EMMA. You are, Charles. Don't let go of my hand.

CHARLES. I'm not going to.

EMMA. Keep walking with me.

The sound of Paris emerges. Doors slide open to reveal images of Paris. JONATHAN enters playing accordian. JOHN picks up a trumpet. JAVIER enters as the VISCOUNT and dances with EMMA. Lights fade.

The End.

THE HOUND OF THE BASKERVILLES
Steven Canny & John Nicholson
Adapted from Arthur Conan Doyle

JEEVES AND WOOSTER IN 'PERFECT NONSENSE'
The Goodale Brothers
Adapted from P.G. Wodehouse

THE JUNGLE BOOK
Stuart Paterson
Adapted from Rudyard Kipling

KENSUKE'S KINGDOM
Stuart Paterson
Adapted from Michael Morpurgo

KES
Lawrence Till
Adapted from Barry Hines

LIONBOY
Marcelo Dos Santos
Adapted from Zizou Corder

NOUGHTS & CROSSES
Dominic Cooke
Adapted from Malorie Blackman

PERSUASION
Mark Healy
Adapted from Jane Austen

THE RAILWAY CHILDREN
Mike Kenny
Adapted from E. Nesbit

SENSE AND SENSIBILITY
Mark Healy
Adapted from Jane Austen

SWALLOWS AND AMAZONS
Helen Edmundson and Neil Hannon
Adapted from Arthur Ransome

A TALE OF TWO CITIES
Mike Poulton
Adapted from Charles Dickens

TREASURE ISLAND
Stuart Paterson
Adapted from Robert Louis Stevenson

THE WOLVES OF WILLOUGHBY CHASE
Russ Tunney
Adapted from Joan Aiken

A Nick Hern Book

The Massive Tragedy of Madame Bovary first published in Great Britain in 2016 as a paperback original by Nick Hern Books Limited, The Glasshouse, 49a Goldhawk Road, London W12 8QP, in association with Peepolykus, Liverpool Everyman & Playhouse, the Nuffield, Southampton, Bristol Old Vic and the Royal & Derngate, Northampton

The Massive Tragedy of Madame Bovary copyright © 2016 John Nicholson and Javier Marzan

John Nicholson and Javier Marzan have asserted their moral right to be identified as the authors of this work

Cover image by Bolland & Lowe

Designed and typeset by Nick Hern Books, London
Printed in Great Britain by CPI Books (UK) Ltd

A CIP catalogue record for this book is available from the British Library

ISBN 978 1 84842 564 4